Bc

ALIVE! AND PAST 65

FRANKLIN M. SEGLER

How to Deal with Aging—for
Families and Church Leaders

BROADMAN PRESS
NASHVILLE, TENNESSEE

© Copyright 1975 • Broadman Press

All rights reserved

4254-14
ISBN: 0-8054-5414-4

Dewey Decimal Classification: 301.43
Library of Congress Catalog Card Number: 74-76690
Printed in the United States of America

To Broadway Baptist Church
a fellowship of ministry
to the whole family of man

CONTENTS

ALIVE! AND PAST 65!

Preface

My first thought after my sixty-fifth birthday was, I am
alive!—and past sixty-five! Why, this is a reason for thanksgiving, a time for celebration. After all, life is a gift from
God, and up to this time it has been very good. What I have
experienced of God up to this present time leads me to believe
that the future will also be full of excitement and meaning.

For several months prior to my retirement from Southwestern Seminary, Fort Worth, Texas, where I had taught
pastoral ministry for twenty-one years, I was concerned about
what I would do in the years after retirement. I thought of
several things—serving as a chaplain in a hospital, working
with a counseling center, serving in the industrial chaplaincy,
and ministering on a church staff as an associate in the area
of pastoral care. While I was pondering this important question, my pastor, John R. Claypool of Broadway Baptist Church,
where I have been a member for twenty-one years, asked me
if I would consider coming on the staff as a minister of pastoral
care. Here was an opportunity for me to return to my first
love, for I was a pastor for nearly twenty years before coming
to teach pastoral ministry in the seminary. I gave thanks to
God for providing this opportunity of ministry at this stage
in life.

My first responsibility in Broadway Church is ministering

to the homebound, in their own homes, in the homes of family members, or in nursing homes. I serve in other areas of ministry wherever I am needed—hospital visitation, conducting funeral services, counseling, preaching occasionally, supervising seminary students in field education, teaching in adult education, working with small groups on occasion, and teaching the Businessmen's Bible Class. Many of these men are retired business and professional men, some advanced in age.

Not long ago an elderly person asked, "Do you think Browning was correct when he said, 'Grow old along with me, the best is yet to be'?" For the first time, she was facing realistically the aging process. I reminded her that Browning gave a basis for those first lines and quoted the entire strophe for her. The poet declared:

> Grow old along with me!
> The best is yet to be,
> The last of life, for which the first was made:
> Our times are in his hand
> Who saith, "A whole I planned,
> Youth shows but half; trust God: see all, nor be afraid!"

Old is beautiful! Or it can be. America is suffering from a youth syndrome. Youth is looked upon as the time of vigor, ambition, hope, challenge, and productivity. Society, including the churches, has placed the emphasis on young people with the view to their becoming successful. Too long we have thought of older people as being past the time of usefulness because they have lost some of their vigor and perhaps are no longer participating in the production of material things.

The American people are now becoming more aware of their growing population of sixty-five or over. In 1850 only 2.5 percent of America's population were sixty-five years of age or more. Today 10 percent—over twenty million persons—belong to this age group. It has been estimated that by the year 2000 there will be at least thirty million Americans over the age of sixty-five.

This fact presents both a challenge and a problem. More senior citizens will be able to share their wisdom and skills as they are released with more time on their hands. On the other hand, more of our people will need better care in their declining years. This challenge must be faced by our entire society and especially our churches.

This book is meant to be more than a "how to do it" manual. It seeks to enter into the deeper experiences that reflect the meaning of life as related to personhood. It is addressed first to persons in the retirement years, those preparing for old age, and to the entire family. It is also a book for pastors and other church leaders who may find in it helpful suggestions for ministering to retired persons.

The progressive levels of life are presented in the context of human experience—individual, family, community, church, and the world. All of us are interrelated and are mutually responsible for one another.

Life can be understood and lived effectively only when it is viewed as a continuous pilgrimage in which each age level is linked to the preceding and succeeding levels. In other words, aging is a lifelong process, and all of us are concerned with it.

When should one start preparing for old age? Why, in one's infancy! That which goes into the experience of the infant will affect his approach to life when he becomes a senior adult.

Your life is your own—a pilgrimage, an unfolding, a project, a becoming. It is never static. Stay alive, be alert, keep on becoming! Paul said, "I have not yet attained, but I press on toward the goal unto the prize of the high calling of God in Christ Jesus."

I welcome you to join me on this journey as we explore the meaning of being alive and past sixty-five. What I will be sharing is partly autobiographical and partly from observation in my participation in the lives of other persons—in my own family, in society in general, and in the church where I am a member. And so, come, grow old along with me. Let us learn to grow old and like it!

Many persons have encouraged me in the writing of this book—colleagues in the ministry, college and seminary teachers, specialists on aging, my own family, and numerous fellow pilgrims among the elderly and homebound—and I hereby express my gratitude.

Seminary students working with the homebound under my supervision in field education have assisted me in clinical studies and encouraged me with their warmth of spirit.

Fannie Mae, my companion of forty years, read the entire manuscript and made many helpful suggestions.

Elizabeth Ferrell typed the manuscript with care and devotion.

Actual names used in the experiences related here have been changed to prevent any embarrassment to the persons involved.

Bible quotations are from the Revised Standard Version unless otherwise indicated. Some passages are a free translation or a paraphrase by the author.

1 My World, and Welcome to It

About three years ago, for the first time, I began seriously considering the meaning of growing old. Oh, I had known for years that I would arrive at this juncture but had not really adjusted my attitudes for the venture. Mandatory retirement was just ahead, and I had to face the reality that I was entering a new era of life.

New questions must be faced. What is life all about? How do human beings experience life in this world? A pastor was asked to speak to the children of his church on what the Bible teaches us about life. He wanted to make it practical and concrete for the children. He told the children, first, the Bible pictures life as getting better and better as it goes along; that is, it is better to be a child than an infant, better to be an adult than an adolescent, better to be aged than an adult. And second, life gets harder and harder as it goes along; that is, it is harder to be a child than an infant, harder to be an adolescent than a child, harder to be an adult than an adolescent, and harder to be aged than an adult.[1]

A Christian doctor, Paul Tournier, said there are two great turning points in life: the passage from childhood to adulthood, and the passage from median adulthood to old age.[2] He quoted Karl Jung: "To refuse to grow old is as foolish as to refuse to leave behind one's childhood." In other words, to leave

13

childhood for adulthood is an adventure, and to enter old age
is also an adventure.

Self-Image

Who am I at this point in time? Today? 1974? Not, who
was I at some time in the past, and not, who will I be ten
years from now. But who am I now?

I recently had an interesting experience which was helpful
in self-understanding. I divided my life into three periods, going
back two-thirds of my present age to twenty-two, then one-
third to forty-four, then now at sixty-six. I asked myself three
questions, applying them to these various sequences: (1) What
was my major interest? (2) What was my major problem? (3)
What was my major hope?

At twenty-two I was a senior in college. My major interests
were completing my education in preparation for pursuing
my chosen vocation in the local church ministry and finding
a suitable companion for marriage. My major problem was
to discover who I was, to arrive at self-identity, and to
strengthen the inner self sometimes referred to by the psychologists as ego strength. My major hope was to find and fulfill
God's plan for my life.

At forty-four years of age in 1951, I was making the transition
from a pastorate of six years in a significant church (Emmanuel
Baptist, Alexandria, Louisiana) to a teaching position at Southwestern Seminary, Fort Worth, Texas. My major interests at
that time were my family (a wife and three children, ages
twelve, nine, and seven) and my vocation. My major problem
was twofold, the illness of my wife (now two years with un-
dulant fever) and the economic burden of providing for family
needs. My major hope was also twofold, to do an effective
job of teaching pastoral ministry in the seminary and to help
my children grow into mature persons.

Now at sixty-six, in the second year of retirement from my teaching position, and a part-time minister of pastoral care at Broadway Baptist Church, my major interest is ministering to persons, particularly to the homebound members of our church, as well as to my own family, in a more sensitive and wiser manner than ever before. My major problem is learning how to adjust to the retirement years, simplifying without dropping out. Change is painful at every stage of life, and the period of senior adulthood is no exception. My major hope is that life may grow richer and more satisfying as it comes to the climax, and that I may continue to serve and glorify God on to the end of life.

Sooner or later every person asks himself, who am I? What is my relation to those about me? To know one's self as a unique and worthwhile person and to be able to share one's uniqueness is a part of the growth process.

The qualities of personhood developed early in life will give one strength for the later phases of life. As Peterson points out, poverty of self before forty intensifies identity crisis for both men and women after forty.[3]

Middle life and the approach to the retirement years is in a sense the culmination of all the efforts and failures in identity formation throughout all the previous years.

What Is Old?

What is old? I once asked a group of girls this question, and I received a number of interesting answers. They replied: being over sixteen is old, when one reaches thirty, the person over fifty, when a person gets gray-headed, when a person has wrinkles, when a person becomes kind and beautiful.

How does one define old age? Dr. Herbert Shore, Executive Director, Golden Acres, a home for Jewish aged, Dallas, Texas, says that aging is a normal process of living and need not be a period of mental and physical deterioration.[4] It can be a time of continuing growth and enrichment for the individual. Each person must accept himself as he is chronologically, as well as biologically, psychologically, and religiously.

There is much misinformation and false understanding about aging. Usually there is a tendency to equate the aging process with a specific number of years—in our culture, sixty-five. This prospect of long life and freedom from work is causing fear of old age, rather than celebration, according to Mrs. Eono J. Harger, a consultant on the problems of aging, associated with the Gerontological Society, Inc. of Washington, D.C.

Mrs. Harger says we need to dispel certain myths that cast a glow over the later years of life. One common mistake is equating the over-sixty-five age bracket with illness. Eighty-five percent of people over sixty-five are not in any way debilitated. Often physical symptoms ascribed to old age are the results of something that happened earlier: sickness, an accident, or bad habits, like smoking and overeating. Neither physical nor mental deterioration occurs with certainty among older people.

Another myth is the idea that people undergo personality change as they grow older. Actually personality traits intensify with age. Tyrants become more tyrannical, loners withdraw more, gregarious people talk more.

Again, it is wrong to accuse older folks of constant reminiscing. Actually, people start recalling their past when they are in their early forties. Many older people keep in touch with life as long as they live and do not revert to mere reminiscing.

Furthermore, not all older people are senile. Senility is not inevitable, and even when it begins to occur, it is sometimes reversible. Proper diet, physical activity, and renewed social contacts can often alleviate what is thought to be senility.

A further myth surrounding aging is the assumption that sexuality dwindles away. Sexual activity continues to be possible and desirable during the entire life span, according to Dr. James A. Peterson.

Another myth presumes that intelligence climaxes at an early age and then begins a long decline. Actually, learning is tied to motivation, and as long as people are motivated, they will keep on learning.

An additional myth, based on nostalgia and romanticism, emphasizes how good it was when grandma and grandpa lived under the same roof with their children and helped to raise the grandchildren. However, it has been pointed out that the three-family unit within one house has rarely been seen in our culture. On the other hand, modern technology, including the telephone and fast transportation, make for more frequent family communication than was possible in other generations. Holidays and special occasions often bring four and five generations together as never before in history.

Coping with Change

Any serious definition of aging must include several aspects of human change. Who am I biologically or physically? A woman may be obsessed with beauty or with being sexually attractive. She may even feel threatened as she faces the period of menopause and leaves the childbearing phase.

A man may be obsessed with physical strength or the virility associated with young manhood. He may feel threatened with the diminishing of the sex drive—afraid he will become impotent and be considered no longer a man.

Physiological change is inevitable. At sixty-six I must acknowledge I do not have the physical strength I possessed at forty or even fifty. To pretend I do is very foolish and perhaps may prompt me to endanger my own health by over-exertion. I must recognize my *physiological age.*

Each individual has also a *chronological age,* which is determined by the number of years he has lived. But his chronological age does not necessarily determine his outlook on life.
One's perspective is colored to some degree by the period
in history in which he grew up. For example, I cannot escape
the influence of the great depression of the early 1930's. I
shall always harbor some anxiety about economic matters as
a result of those lean years.

Then there is the *psychological age* indicated by how old
a person feels and acts. In reality, each person experiences
these three different ages all at once, the physiological, the
chronological, and the psychological. All three interact and
cannot be considered separately.

Overarching all of life is one's *religious age* or state of
spiritual maturity. Who am I in relation to God and his purposes for my life? After all, in these later years "we walk
by faith and not by sight" (2 Cor. 5:7).

There are psychological laws of aging one must accept if
he is to continue to achieve satisfaction in the senior years.
Ethel Sabin Smith suggests the following laws: The continuity
of selfhood; a fundamental ability to enjoy oneself; modification
and following mature ways of striving; an understanding of
time in facing life and death with equanimity. All growth
involves relinquishment as well as acquisition, knowing what
to give up and what to keep.

Most important of all, a person must be certain of his own
worth in old age. Smith concludes, "If he knows that in old
age he has a role to play as vital and as demanding as any
he assumed in his prime, he will be able to take the last curtain
call with dignity and satisfaction, with the applause of his
admirers breaking upon his ears." [5]

Whole Life Cycle

I can understand myself at this stage of life only if I see my personhood in relation to my entire biographical experience from birth to death. Erik Erickson speaks of identity in the life cycle in eight stages: (1) infancy—basic trust versus basic mistrust; (2) ages 2-3—autonomy versus shame and doubt; (3) ages 4-5—initiative versus guilt; (4) middle childhood—industry versus inferiority; (5) adolescence—identity versus role confusion; (6) young adulthood—intimacy versus isolation; (7) adulthood—generativity versus stagnation; and (8) maturity—ego integrity versus despair.

Each stage of life is involved with crisis and conflict, and the struggle to meet the problems encountered. In the retirement years these problems may include, as noted by Havighurst, decreasing physical strength and health; retirement and reduced income; death of one's spouse; establishing an explicit affiliation with one's age group; meeting social and civic obligations; establishing satisfactory physical living arrangements.

The line of distinction which marks off middle life from old age is as distinct as that line which marks off childhood from adolescence. It varies greatly between individuals. A person might be fifty years old chronologically, much older biologically, with one or more organs in his body nearly worn out, but younger psychologically, in the sense that he has not lived very far out into the stream of life.

Preparation for the later years must begin in infancy and continue throughout life. It has been said that by the age of fifty a man is either a fool or a philosopher. Oliver Wendell Holmes said, "To be seventy years young is sometimes far more cheerful and hopeful than to be forty years old."

In a report to the 1971 White House Conference on Aging,

the group for the advancement of psychiatry stated: "We believe that the study and understanding of one segment of the life cycle helps the understanding of the other parts of the cycle, but life is of one piece, to be valued from birth to death."

Meaning of Personhood

In order to age successfully a person has to know who he is, the nature of his personhood. Man is multidimensional. He is more than his component parts. He is a unitary person. He is biochemical, psychosocial, and of divine image. Beyond the physical and psychological is the ultimate or spiritual dimension, the level of transcendence in which man is related to the Divine. Made in the image of God, who is infinite mystery, man is also mystery in the depths of his being. We must take off the masks of appearance and get to the core of the person, as Tournier has reminded us in *The Meaning of Persons.*

A human being experiences as a unit, not as a fragmented person. He is a sensory, thinking, feeling, faithing person. He experiences through his body, his intellect, his emotions, his will, and his spirit. He is never mere body, or mind, or emotions, or will. He is more than the sum total of these various elements.

At different times various aspects of the personality may be uppermost, but all are always a part of experience. In his book *The Secret of Radiant Life* W. E. Sangster suggests that the profoundest philosopher is never only thinking, the most ardent lover is never only feeling, the most determined militarist is never only willing, and the maturest Christian is never only faithing. All aspects of personality are always present in some degree.

Who are you? You are an individual. No two persons are

alike. Roger J. Williams, professor of biochemistry at the University of Texas, wrote a book entitled *You Are Extraordinary*. He says that every person is distinct in every particular, from his fingerprints to his stomach, his heart, his brain, and his nervous system. You are you because God has made you who you are. You are extraordinary, and you are significant. God has no one else like you in his world.

The older person can learn to live with himself—his potentialities and his limitations. He can learn to live with his fellowman. He can learn to live with God, in whom he lives and moves and has his being.

Accepting Reality

If a person is to grow old gracefully, he must accept the process of aging realistically. There can be no pretense, no fantasizing about one's own age. Change is happening to me. The world is changing, and I figure I had better accept it with its changes if I am to be a part of it. Future shock in the real world of ongoing history is preferable to crystallization of the past—which can lead only to apathy and deterioration.

Schulz offers both truth and humor in his *Peanuts* characters. One day "psychiatrist" Lucy challenged Charlie Brown, "Do you have a room of your own?" "Yes, I have a room of my own. Why do you ask?" "Do you realize that you won't always have your own room? Someday you will go away to college or get married, and your room will no longer be your own." With wrinkled brow Charlie asked, "Why are you telling me these things?" Lucy replied, "Well, I'm making a list, and I'm heading it, 'Things you may as well know.' "

Can I accept myself where I am in today's world? Do I have a philosophy of life which includes a proper perspective on aging and the climax of life? If I do, then at every age level I must do that which will enhance, strengthen, develop, and enrich my personhood and honor the Creator.

My aging friend, this is your world. Paul once said, "All are yours; and ye are Christ's; and Christ is God's" (1 Cor. 3:22-23). This is your space—the place you occupy is a gift, your life-space to use, to relate to. This is your world of persons, a world of relationships. You are part of the human family. This is your world of divine realities. Relate to God and to these realities. Accept and affirm these gifts!

Ross Snyder says we are called to actualize life, to bring off a life world, to be a cocreator in this world.[6] God is always doing a new thing with you and for you, if you will only allow him to do it; and this is true in every stage of life. Accept responsibility for becoming what God wants you to become. You are an agent of life.

Do not be a senior dropout. The most dangerous of all attitudes is apathy, a sort of not caring, a "dropping out" of life. See it through. Look for meaning in life. Respond with feeling, be it anger or gratitude. Do not just sit there. Respond! As the young people say, "Tune in, and turn on!"

The threat of nonbeing and the courage to be are a paradox we all experience. Therefore, choose life. And remember the length of life is not our primary concern. The quality of life is more important than mere quantity. Gerontologists are more concerned with making life more livable in the senior years than they are in merely prolonging it.

Old Is Beautiful

Yes, old can be beautiful. Some of the most charming persons I know are in the latter decades of life. My own mother was still teaching a Bible class of older women when she was eighty years of age. Or, look at Helen Hayes, for example. She refuses to quit growing or lose interest. I heard Robert Frost quote some of his poetry from memory when he was past seventy-five years of age. His eyes sparkled and flashed, and a smile traced across his face as he shared with feeling some of those nuggets of truth learned from experience.

What is my self-image? Is it adequate? If God made me in his image, and he did, then I am important. If God gave me his love and redeemed me through Jesus Christ his Son, and he did, then I must love myself because I am loved of God.

As I survey my life, I must be honest to acknowledge my humanity, my finitude, and my failures. I also must add up the achievements and the goals that have been reached. I must acknowledge myself as a man in Christ, a man for whom Christ died, a man for whom God has purpose and meaning. Who I am is more important than anything I do. All activity is designed to support the growth and fulfillment of the person. Whatever makes me more like God is good.

In Auden's Christmas oratorio "For the Time Being," the three wise men recall why they are following the star.

The first wise man: to discover how to be truthful now is the reason I follow this star.

Second wise man: to discover how to be living now is the reason I follow this star.

Third wise man: to discover how to be loving now is the reason I follow this star.

The three together: to discover how to be human now is the reason we follow this star.

Specialists on aging hope to make life better in the later years. Research encourages them to believe they can hold back physical ravages of senescence, and perhaps abolish many of the hazards of old age altogether. They do not particularly want to stretch out the years of senility, keep people alive in a state of helpless decrepitude, prolong the years of child-hood, as has been done in experimenting with rats through restrictive feeding; prolong life by inducing periods of hibernation during which a person would continue to exist in a state of suspended animation. They want "to extend the number of continuous years spent at a productive and enjoyable level of health and intellectual power." [7]

Someone has written:

> Nobody grows old by merely living a number of years;
> People grow old only by deserting their ideals.
> Years wrinkle the skin, but self-distrust, fear and despair—
> Those are the long, long years that bow the head and
> Turn the growing spirit back to dust.
> You are as young as your faith,
> As old as your doubt;
> As young as your self-confidence,
> As old as your fear;
> As young as your hope,
> As old as your despair.

2 *I've Family, Too*

It is good to have experienced life in a multigenerational family setting. Some of my earliest memories were enjoyable relationships with my own grandparents. We always loved to go over the hills and far away to grandfather's house on Thanksgiving—or any other time. Grandparents were something special to us, and their farm homes were always full of warmth and exhilaration.

As soon as we had children of our own, Fannie Mae and I sought to keep them in touch with our parents, to let them know that their grandparents were a part of our family too. Then, when we became grandparents, our children faithfully brought their children to visit us and their great-grandparents also.

In the days when America was largely an agrarian population, the extended family included the grandparents who originally purchased the farmland. Then it was shared with their children. And when they became adults and married, the grandchildren participated in the same farmland. Perhaps other farms were bought or rented next to Grandpa's farm. Uncles and aunts, nephews, nieces, and cousins all felt they were part of one another. What concerned the grandparents, concerned the adult parents and the grandchildren. If one was sick, all were concerned. If one had a birthday, all found some reason for rejoicing; they all celebrated together. This was the life of the extended family.

The social structures of America have changed rapidly in the past generation. Sociologists are now talking about the nuclear family composed only of an adult couple and one or more children. Technological advances have taken family members into various parts of their own country and over the entire world. These trends have isolated nuclear families—fathers, mothers, children—living far from relatives and friends in houses or apartments, chosen of necessity, and not because they love the location or have good reasons for taking roots.

Dr. Margaret Mead, noted anthropologist, says there is an urgent need to reestablish multigeneration families. Many other sociologists and psychologists have thrown up their hands in surrender. They claim the day of the extended family is gone. However, home is still the first unit of society and absolutely essential for the preservation of ultimate values. Love and devotion, character and purpose are learned and shared together by old and young alike.

Biblical Foundations

Early in Genesis God said it was not good for man to be alone, and he created for him a companion. As the Bible story unfolds, the family is seen to be the first unit of society ordained by God. One of the ten commandments says, "Honor your father and your mother," and it was considered so important it was the first commandment to which God added a promise—"that your days may be long upon the land which the Lord your God gives you."

God commanded the first couple to go forth and replenish the earth. Children were considered a blessing, and older people were considered God's gift to the children.

The Old Testament exhorted society to honor older people: "You shall rise up before the hoary head, and honor the face of the old man and fear your God; I am the Lord" (Lev. 19:32). "Hearken unto your father who begot you, and do not despise your mother when she is old" (Prov. 23:22).

The story of Abraham and his sons and the sons of Jacob is filled with romance and respect for family. In ancient times older people were honored and revered among the Hebrews, the Egyptians, the Greeks, and the Romans. Severe penalties were imposed when the young neglected or failed to show respect for older people.

The philosopher Plato said, "We can obtain no more honorable possession from the gods than fathers and forefathers worn down with age, and mothers who have undergone the same change, whom when we delight, God is pleased with the honor; and everyone that is governed by right understanding fears and reverences them."

The New Testament continues this exhortation concerning older persons. Paul urged, "Honor your father and mother; which is the first commandment with promise; that it may be well with you and you may live long on the earth" (Eph. 6:2-3). Paul wrote Timothy, "If any widow has children or grandchildren, let them first learn to show piety toward their own family, and to requite their parents: for this is acceptable in the sight of God" (1 Tim. 5:4). Throughout the Bible it is assumed that old and young are mutually responsible for one another.

Musings of a Grandfather

As an older person, how do I relate to my family? Am I able to fit into the growing, changing family? I would like to be a helpful companion to my wife, the right kind of parent to my own adult children, and a warm and loving grandfather. What can I expect from my family—all of them? You see, I am really a part of the family and hope to remain close to them as long as I live.

Family relationships in old age are built upon foundations of past experiences and relationships. When do you start preparing for old age? Why, when you are born into the human family.

For example, I was born to good parents. Share-cropper farmers, they were poor in this world's goods, but rich in natural endowments as persons. And they were rich in love. There were six of us children, and there was enough love to go around. We learned to work hard and share with other persons in the family.

Also, we learned early the meaning of family tragedy and crisis. Our father was killed in an accident when I was ten years old. The other four brothers and one sister ranged in age from eight years to three months. Mother was twenty-nine. For six years she was a lone parent, except for father substitutes we found in our uncles. We moved near grandfather's old farm to a farm of our own which they rented for us.

And we enjoyed our grandfather. He was a hard worker, a good disciplinarian, and very wise. He was also kind, and patient, and jolly, which helped lonely growing boys find joy in living. Grandmother Gabriel died before we had the privilege of knowing her.

I was fortunate to marry a good wife who has been an excellent companion, always sharing life at every level, including the crises. God blessed us with two sons and a daughter. Now they are married, and we have five grandchildren. Perhaps it will not be many years until I shall be a great-grandfather!

Bridging the Generation Gap

One grandfather remarked that it was rather startling when he first observed his own sideburns were longer than those of his grandson's. A grandmother who prides herself in being able to communicate with her grandchildren remarked, "What does hair length have to do with it? The main thing is the attitude, and I find that our grandsons have as good outlook as we did when we were their age."

The stimulating newspaper columnist Sydney J. Harris reported that one of the nicest compliments any of his children ever paid him came from his middle daughter just before she left for college. They were talking about "age," about being young and being old. She remarked, "I am glad you act your age and don't try to compete with the new youth culture." "You don't think of me as 'old' do you," he asked. She answered, "Not at all. I don't think of you as young or old, but as kind of—timeless."

If both youth and elders could think of life as being timeless, they would achieve understanding and bridge the so-called generation gap. The spirit of timelessness will include all periods of life—infancy, adolescence, and maturity—and old age, the summation of all of life. Harris observed, "To forget what it was like to be young, to fall out of sympathy with the 'new youth' is to grow rotten before you grow ripe." To be timeless is better than to be young or old or any other specific age. This is what living is all about.

Understanding Older Family Members

A person does not become someone else as he grows older. He has the same basic needs and traits that he had when he was younger. One daughter wisely recognized, "Mother is like she always was, only more so." It takes a great deal

of insight for children and grandchildren to understand grandparents. It also requires effort to relate to them and, while
living with them, permit them to be themselves.

A spirit of mutual concern and understanding is essential
to keep family relationships strong. In his book *Married Love
in the Middle Years,* Peterson suggests there are five C's which
form the basis for growth in family relationships: curiosity,
creativeness, comprehension, compassion, and commitment.
In other words, if family members are to grow together, they
will need openness, imagination, understanding of the facts,
a spirit of love and tenderness, and a commitment to one
another "till death do us part."

William Poe suggests that younger generations should try
putting themselves in the place of elderly persons.[1] Imagine
you had lost your teeth, half your eyesight, a part of your
hearing, and more than half your ability to move around
quickly. In addition, you are anxious about becoming a burden,
losing your ability to look after your business affairs, not having
enough money to pay your bills, and uncertain where you
ought to live. It is only good sense to acknowledge there are
new limitations and problems in the older years which call
for family understanding and support.

Older people generally do not like change. They have been
accustomed to a routine and find it difficult to make adjustments. Changes have to come, but we should help them adjust
with as little shock as possible. Patience and consideration,
rather than forcing change upon them, will make life more
pleasant for all concerned.

Older persons have emotional needs just as younger persons
do. They need to be accepted as members of the family. They
need to be loved and to give love. They are particularly
sensitive to rejection. They like to be treated with seriousness
and not merely indulged. Grandmother will notice when she

is slighted. She wants her ideas considered, and her wishes heard.

Grandmother Thurgood was not able to attend the wedding of her granddaughter, but the bride and groom took time to pay her a visit before leaving on their honeymoon. Later, as I visited in her home, she kept saying over and over, "I'll never forget those young people for taking time out to make me happy."

Our elderly parents also need to be accepted physically. Physical presence means more than all the words showered upon them. Inviting them to be physically present for family gatherings, or to go to them when they cannot come to you, is a part of family obligation. To reject them physically is often interpreted as total personal rejection.

Financial security is one of the greatest needs of older people. They are fortunate indeed if they have an adequate income to care for all their physical comforts. To be free of money cares is perhaps the best medicine an old person can have. If elderly parents do not have sufficient income of their own, their children and grandchildren should see that they have a fixed amount available to them each month. This will give them a feeling of independence, self-respect, and freedom to purchase what they desire, so long as their money holds out.

Life's greatest needs are spiritual. The inner man must continually be renewed if life is to have meaning. The most important questions of life are theological. They have to do with ultimate meaning. They are particularly significant for older people. Toward the end of life's pilgrimage, they begin to ask seriously: How long will I live? Why must I give up my companion? Why do good people suffer? What will it be like to die? Is there life beyond the grave? Will I be with my wife (or husband) in heaven?

Younger persons should not feel threatened when talking about death with older people. Let them talk: learn to listen. Sometimes it is like a confessional which lifts burdens and gives peace to the soul. To understand that death is simply an event in the midst of life and be able to discuss it openly is a healthy condition for the entire family.

Young people, with their normal intellectual doubts and questionings, should be careful not to take lightly the sincere beliefs and deep convictions of grandfather or grandmother. Ridicule may wound the spirit to the point that it is almost beyond healing.

How to Be an Elderly Parent or Grandparent

Like parenting, grandparenting must be learned. Learning can take place only if there is openness and desire for new insights. We older persons have a tendency to be set in our ways and to think we are always right. Our children and grandchildren have much to teach us if we will only remain teachable.

Older parents must realize their own children are now adults and have families of their own and must be granted the privilege of making their own decisions. We should be slow to give advice but ready to share when our opinions are desired.

Sometimes it is necessary to recognize the reversal of roles in relationships between parents and adult children. In other words, it may be necessary to permit our own children to parent us at times. They may be in a position to know what is best for us and offer good counsel in the solution of our problems. For example, Fannie Mae and I mentioned the possibility of selling our home and moving into an apartment. All three of our children advised us to keep the home since we enjoy it so much.

The younger adult generation have heavy responsibilities.

They are busy producing and meeting the financial obligations of the family. Their minds are absorbed with problems of their own children. They have priorities which demand their attention and time. They are limited in the amount of time and energy they can share with their parents.

Older parents should not be too demanding. I knew one elderly mother who expected her son or daughter-in-law to call her every day at a certain hour. If they failed to do so, she felt slighted, and retaliated by pouting. This made it unpleasant for the entire family.

The grandparent must learn to take second place, or even third place, in the family. Along about Christmas time, Mrs. Moore said, "Of course, we enjoy having the children and grandchildren and great-grandchildren home for Christmas day. However, they have their own children and grandchildren and sometimes like to stay home on Christmas. That doesn't suit me the best, but I know it's best for them. We've had our time, and so we do not want to expect too much from our children and grandchildren. They usually try to drop by sometime during the holidays. After all, one day is as good as another to celebrate when you have your loved ones.

Time has always been the thief in the parent-child relationship. Responsibilities of the young family demand so much of the parents' time that before they realize it, the children are gone, and they have not given them the time they intended to. This is one contribution grandparents can make. They do have time to enjoy their grandchildren and to share love with them. A grandson will appreciate being invited to help with the gardening or go on a little fishing trip. A granddaughter always considers it a privilege to help grandmother make cookies or design a doll dress. One picture I'll always cherish: our little four-year-old granddaughter with flour all over her dress from helping grandmother make sugar cookies, which she passed around to all of us.

Wise grandparents will have a box of toys for the grand-children when they come to visit. Then there are story books and picture books galore which always make it a joy to visit at the grandparents' house.

Grandmother's cooking is always a treat. This is especially true if she remembers their favorite dishes. There are other little ways to make grandchildren happy. Invite one grandchild at a time to visit so that you can give him all your attention. Treat him as an equal. Carry on a genuine conversation with him. Let him do the things that he cannot experience at home, the things his parents do not have time to do.

Grandchildren appreciate compliments concerning school, accomplishments, musical achievements, development in manners, and general characteristics of maturing. They especially enjoy participating in little chores, such as breaking string beans, feeding the dog, setting the table, hammering a nail, or even using a paint brush.

As someone has said, investing time in grandchildren brings immediate dividends of joy to three generations. Furthermore, it is a growth investment, a rich endowment, which will become a part of life throughout the years to come. These riches of warmth and wisdom and human sharing are often passed down from one generation to another.

Economic Help from Children

My wife's parents were of sturdy, stable heritage, honest, hardworking, trustworthy. Her father was never unemployed. At the turn of the century he started out as a farmer and made a good living for his wife and three children. Later he had a grocery store. Then he worked for the public in the city, the county, the state. When he retired, after eighteen years of service in a state prison system, he immediately found a job driving a delivery truck for a laundry and cleaners. He worked there until he was eighty-three. His wife also worked as a hospital receptionist during the depression years to help send the children to college.

When the retirement years came, there was not much to live on, for they had been generous and unselfish with their income, spending it all on others. As we began to help them financially, the proud, independent, hardworking father at first rebelled. "I don't want to be dependent on others and create problems for them," he said more than once. One day I suggested, "What we are doing is not a gift. It is your investment coming back to you. You earned it through the years and invested it in your children and grandchildren. It is now a privilege for us to return a part of it. Please do not ever hesitate to accept our help." He seemed to find it a little easier after that.

Financial help should be planned in a systematic way— regular monthly checks for elderly parents to be used as they see fit. There should be no strings attached. If they have a regular budget to live on, they will feel good about being able to spend it for themselves.

It is usually wise for children to inquire occasionally whether their parents are able to meet the bills. As they grow older, it may even be good sometimes to offer help with their bookkeeping. One mother in her eighties will often call her daughter and say, "My checkbook is all fouled up. I can't seem to make it balance. The next time you come I hope you will double-check it for me." Help is always appreciated when it is asked for.

Before parents reach the state of senility and incapacitation, it is good for all financial problems to be worked out so that younger adults may take care of business affairs. It is often wise for power of attorney to be granted to someone who can handle such responsibilities, just in case.

A Growing Companionship

In his delightful book *To Understand Each Other* Paul Tournier says that understanding has to be achieved by continuous effort on the part of marriage partners. This is true of older persons who have spent many years together, for they should never take each other for granted. There are always depths in the mystery of personhood which call for openness and exploration.

When I pause to think deeply and imaginatively about my wife Fannie Mae as a person, after nearly forty years of a good life together, I am increasingly aware of depths I cannot fathom, of qualities which mature with the years. And my appreciation for her grows continually.

If we are to achieve understanding at any age in marriage, we need to express ourselves, to keep openness and honesty at the center. We need courage to expose ourselves to each other, not pretending or hiding our feelings. Then, we need to cultivate love, to keep the romance in marriage. Courtship's curiosity must not be lost.

Husbands and wives need to accept their natural differences as persons—activist versus meditative, extrovert versus introvert, intuitive versus logician, feminine versus masculine. All these qualities should serve to complement, rather than compete with one another, particularly when persons grow older.

Even in affection and love there are different qualities in husband and wife. One important way of expressing love is sexual activity. To understand the sexual feelings and needs of one's partner calls for a lifetime of concern and effort. As physical and emotional changes come with aging, sensitive companions will seek to understand and try to meet the needs of each other.

Psychologist James Peterson says the ability to share in sex life does not cease in old age. It may wane some, but it can still be a vital part of marriage. This is an important way to express love even in old age.

A medical doctor told of counseling with a couple past eighty who still enjoyed this intimate relationship. This act of sharing is not as intense but is still normal and gratifying. Actually, it is essential for personal fulfillment as long as one is physically well.

Lewis Sherrill counsels that when sex is shared out of genuine love, it is not dependent upon the physical and sensual. The waning of the sensory does not produce panic where there is love, for love is "deeper, wider, and longer" than sex. "Love is eternal rejoicing in the body of the beloved, yet not decaying with the decay of the body, nor dying with its physical death. Love abideth." [2]

After all, when love prevails, we want to help each other find joy and fulfillment throughout life. And the capacity for joy and understanding should grow as long as life lasts. Tournier suggests that in mature love, the past, the present, and the future are woven into a garment fitting for eternity.

Under One Roof?

One of the main concerns of the family is that older people may have a comfortable place to live. It is generally agreed that a separate home for active old people is the ideal. Usually both the older and younger generations are happier when they can live separately. However, circumstances have to govern this decision. Sometimes it is necessary and even desirable for two or more generations to live together.

Dr. Poe lists several of these situations:

When elders are advanced in age and have suffered a deterioration in mental alertness or physical capabilities.

The husband or wife has died and the survivor is not able to deal with the problem or is unwilling to live alone.

It may be financially impractical or impossible to maintain a home for just one person.

There may be fear that injury or illness might come suddenly to the individual with no one present to handle an emergency.

Medical or nursing care may be essential for the individual, and this is impossible when the parent is living alone.

Ablebodied grandparents may be needed to take care of the home of children and grandchildren, especially when parents must work or when there is illness in the family.[3]

Arrangement of living quarters is very important. A separate house for the elderly parent or parents is the ideal. I am acquainted with one family in which the elderly mother has her own little house back of her daughter's home. She has her own things in the house, and enjoys the privilege of running it to suit herself. She is available to come and stay in the larger house and to assist with family responsibilities at times. Precautions have been taken to make her home safe and livable. There are no throw rugs, the bathtub is equipped with a handrail, the bed is firm and comfortable, and heating and cooling facilities are adequate.

When a separate house is not available, a private room should be designated for elderly parents. It will be their room to decorate and furnish as they please. Furthermore, they need privacy and independence. A separate bath is essential so that they will not feel they are interfering with the family.

The household should be organized so as to indicate the responsibilities and roles of all members involved. A division of labor can be made clear so that every person will feel he is making some contribution.

The entire family will attempt to cooperate and not interfere with the plans of one another. Elderly parents enjoy their own television and do not necessarily expect to spend all the evenings in the living room with the rest of the family. Times for visiting in their room as well as in the general family room may be desirable. However, the privacy of both families should be respected.

Grandparents must remember that discipline is primarily the responsibility of the parents and not the grandparents. They should never indulge the grandchildren when it is contrary to the wishes of the parent. They ought never add their two cents worth when family discussions are in progress. It is a wise grandparent who knows when to speak and when not to speak.

As our parents grow old, we find it increasingly difficult to keep them comfortable and to meet their needs. We may develop guilt feelings because we can't do all we desire to do for them. We should acknowledge reality and not blame ourselves when we have done all we can.

My own mother lived to be eighty-one, and she insisted on living in her own house to the end. Seven living children often offered to take her in, but she loved her independence. Then one day what we feared happened. She died of a massive heart attack in her sleep, alone in her own home. No, not really alone. This manner of death she had desired and prayed for. Two children lived nearby and checked on her every day. Her family doctor said nothing could have been done for her, even if someone had been present.

Although we wished someone had been there, our best judgment told us we had not been negligent. And mother lived life joyfully to the end. She taught her Sunday School class Sunday, had been active Monday, went to bed feeling good that night, and woke up in heaven the next morning. She always knew she had a vital place in her family.

3 *Alive in Church and Community*

An elderly church member recently said, "I wish our church would show the same interest in its senior adults it shows in its young people. The leaders are always planning something for our youth, and I am for that. I wouldn't want us to do any less for our young people. They are the future of our church. But why do they forget the older church members who are the past heritage and often the present strength of our church?"

I agreed this is a legitimate observation. And I appreciated the spirit in which it was given. There was no bitterness or jealousy indicated—just a longing to be understood and appreciated and useful. This neglect seems to be rather widespread among our churches. It is due in part to a lack of knowledge concerning the needs, as well as the potential, of older persons in the church. Sometimes it is due also to misconceptions about senior adults—their desires, needs, attitudes, abilities, energies, and contributions to the life of church and community.

Need for Understanding

In a minister's workshop, "The Church and the Aging," sponsored jointly by the Texas Research Institute of Mental Sciences, Texas Medical Center, Houston, and the Texas Conference of Churches, a survey revealed that many church leaders have limited understanding about the aging process. Indeed, some are guilty of encouraging a spirit of "age-ism."

The following generalizations and myths indicated rather limited understanding:

(1) It would probably be better if most old people lived in residential units with people their own age.

(2) People always grow wiser with the coming of old age.

(3) Most old people are irritable, grouchy, and unpleasant.

(4) Most old people make one feel ill-at-ease.

(5) Most old people are capable of new adjustments when the situation demands it.

(6) Most old people are cheerful, agreeable, and good-natured.

(7) Most old people tend to let their homes become shabby and unattractive.

(8) Old people are unable to change.

(9) In general, most old people are alike.

(10) Most old people make excessive demands for love and reassurance.

Of course, some of these concepts are true of some older persons. However, many of these ideas show a lack of discernment. The church needs to dispel myths and fallacies, as well as increase knowledge, in order to help change attitudes about the aging process.

A Theology of Aging

Someone has observed that the church is elderly. We talk about the future of the church being in the hands of the young, but it is now actually in the hands of the old. Most church memberships are made up largely of older people. The church as a pilgrim people is still on the way to becoming what God has redeemed it to become. Therefore, the older members as well as the young must stay alive in their personal faith, their convictions, their activie ministries, their mutual support and fellowship, and their witnessing to the world outside the church.

Man, created in the image of God, is significant in every era of his life pilgrimage. The church must see the image of God in the face of the infant, in the wonderment of the child, in the curiosity of the youth, in the productivity of the adult, and in the wisdom of the senior adult. A human being is meant to become more like the image of God toward the climax of life than he ever has been during his pilgrimage.

The church should shape its ministry for the whole family of man and provide an opportunity for all its members to participate in its fellowship, from the cradle to the grave. One church set forth its philosophy of ministry in the following statement:

It is the aim of this church to make religion
As considerate of persons as the New Testament
As devoted to justice as the Old Testament prophets
As responsive to truth as science
As beautiful as art
As intimate as the home
As indispensable as the air we breathe.

No distinction is made as to age groupings in this objective. Consideration for persons is all-inclusive. This speaks to the basic dignity of every life. All have a need for belonging. There is a continuity to life that cannot be divided by the arbitrary lines marked off by age groupings.

As people grow older, inner needs do not change. The spiritual needs of the aging are those of every person written large—the need for identity, meaning, love, wisdom, and fulfillment. The person continues to grow in relation to God as

long as he is open to the graces God offers and as long as
he continues a sharing relationship with the people of God.

Pearl S. Buck once remarked that "young" and "old" are
meaningless words except as we use them to denote where
we are in the process at this stage of being. For her, life was
an ongoing process, and she kept on making her contribution
through her God-given ability to write, even when she was
past three-score years and ten.

The Interpreter's House

There is a retreat for ministers in a certain mountain area
called "The Interpreter's House." The purpose of this center
is to provide continuing education and growth for ministers
whose work sometimes grinds them down and hinders them
from becoming God's servants in reality. The approach is
contemporary and relevant for life today. Leaders at the center
make use of all the knowledge available for revitalizing life—
theological, psychological, sociological, and cosmic.

In a sense, the church should be "The Interpreter's House"
for its maturing adults, as well as all other age levels. People
need preparation for aging. The church can provide the opportunity.

People need help to interpret the meaning of life. In *The
Struggle Of the Soul* Lewis J. Sherrill follows the pilgrimage
of the human self through its various stages or types of experience, from the beginning to the end. He uses three symbolic
terms to clarify the meaning of life. He sees life as a *tread-
mill*—no meaning, monotonous, a weary grind. Life may also
be viewed as a *saga* or *epic* such as the hero in Homer's
Odyssey. The biblical symbol for interpreting the meaning
of life is the *pilgrimage*—human existence consciously related
to God who lifts life to the divine level. Life is seen in both
the vertical and horizontal dimensions. On this pilgrimage the

individual's life is interpreted in relationship to nature, other persons, and God.

The church can help maturing adults keep love alive by including them in its fellowship. They are a part of the church family, as important as any other age group. They have much warmth to give, and they need warmth from other persons.

It is easy for middle and older adults to feel used up and sometimes to become disillusioned and discouraged. The church can help challenge them to the adventure of living. Paul Tournier says that adventure is an instinct peculiar to man.[1] All human enterprises start in the exciting fever of discovery. As they become more organized, they formulate standardization. Then they become commonplace, a matter of mere routine, and soon the joy of adventure has gone out of them. Human beings must find new channels to revitalize life. The spirit of adventure may be choked, smothered, and repressed, but it never disappears from the human personality. Man experiences phases of growth, and the last phase or climax should still be adventure.

The church can help adults understand the meaning of persons and the changes that come at the different levels of life. If they understand these changes, they will be better prepared to meet them. Preparation for aging is a lifelong process. All the church's members mutually help one another understand life at its various stages. The older person, who learns to accept change gracefully, not only experiences more tranquility of spirit and a feeling of fulfillment but is also prepared to be a better servant of God and his fellowman.

Church leaders are called of God to be enablers and facilitators. One pastor constantly reminds his fellow church members that he is not called to do all their work for them. He does hope and pray that he may be an enabler, helping them prepare for ministry by finding the proper motivation in a continuing pilgrimage. Staff members, with all their expertise and training, are not paid to do the church's work for its members. They are charged to be facilitators, calling people forth, helping them find the places where their particular talents are needed, and giving them guidance and support as they participate in Christian ministry. Senior adults will respond to this kind of challenge.

O Worship the Lord

One day I was visiting with an eighty-five-year-old man in the hospital. Toward the end of the visit, he suggested that I read something from the Bible. I turned to Psalm 121, "I lift up mine eyes to the hills. From whence does my help come? My help comes from the Lord, who made heaven and earth." He responded, "Actually, we have no other place to turn. I really miss the worship services in our church and will be glad when I can again go to the house of the Lord."

Public worship experiences are cherished by older adults. Regular attendance at worship has become habitual with them. They feel with the psalmist, "As the hart pants after the water brook, so pants my soul after thee, O God." They really do hunger and thirst for the living God.

As people grow older, they particularly love the celebrative aspects of worship. They have grown in their understanding of the nature of God, and they delight to adore and praise him. Prayers of adoration and thanksgiving now exceed prayers of petition.

Church leaders, in planning music for worship, should remember the senior adults as well as the young people. There is something solid about the great hymns which exalt the attributes of God and dwell upon the great theological themes. Older persons are strengthened by the rich heritage which hymns of the fathers provide for them.

Older adults, who are gifted in music, find it difficult to give up their place in the choir. As long as their voices blend and do not distract, they ought to be encouraged to participate in the organized choir program. The younger generations of the church should make them feel welcome and indeed learn to profit from their warmth and maturity. Senior adults must be prepared to relinquish their places in the choir when they no longer are an asset. Honesty, courtesy, and gentleness on the part of leaders will help them make the change.

Prayer is of the very essence of worship. The more experience people have in prayer, the more meaningful it becomes to them. Older adults are among the greatest pray-ers in the church. They appreciate being included in the prayers, and many of them will be pleased to participate in leading public prayers. The genuineness of their prayers, refined in the fires of many experiences, may often bring the congregation into the very presence of God.

Preaching to meet people's needs is the aim of every concerned pastor. People over sixty-five years of age represent a large portion of the congregations who listen to sermons. As they prepare their messages, pastors have an important responsibility to the old as well as the young. Edgar N. Jackson says preaching to the aged calls for an understanding of their special needs. Their fear of exclusion from the life they have known, increased limitation in strength, the diminishing circle of friends, the demands for the reordering of life, and the deep spiritual needs they experience cry out for preaching which speaks to their condition. As they approach the end of life, they are more concerned about the ultimate and eternal values. They are often realistic about death and appreciate help in preparing for the last mile of the journey. Sometimes they have moods of depression which call for reassurance and support.

Some young preachers have a tendency to use contemporary words and clichés, and to avoid biblical imagery, in an attempt to be relevant to the younger generation. Jackson urges us to build into the context of the sermons those words, phrases, and illustrations that make older persons feel a sense of "at homeness."

Leslie Weatherhead, whose long ministry in London endeared him to many generations, made four specific points in a sermon to older people: The older years are as normal as any other years, and God's invitations are as pertinent as ever. Then, older people should honestly face the demands of change and not fight against inevitable reality. Furthermore, older members should realize the assets of their years. They have a mature wisdom which they can share with younger generations. Finally, we need to think about death and prepare for it as a normal experience. We should not become preoccupied with it but develop an understanding of the processes involved, such as the relation of spring and summer, autumn and winter.

People Who Care

Older Christians care about other people. Because they care, they are willing to minister. The mutual care of souls in the church is never more pertinent than when it includes the senior adults. People who have known many years have suffered and learned much from life. In the fires of pain many have developed a mellowness, a sweetness, a sensitivity, and a concern for other people who suffer.

Because of this preparation, they often make ideal ministers in the church's care of souls. They should be encouraged to participate in pastoral care. They may hesitate to volunteer their services, but are usually willing to respond when leaders in the church request their ministry. They usually make ex-

cellent visitors. Many can also assist in transportation and other
ministries.

Often the best counselors are those who have known much
counsel. I knew an elderly minister's wife, with snow-white
hair and a smile on her face, who related well to young people.
Because of her openness and love, they often came to her
for wise counsel.

Elders as Leaders

In the New Testament churches some of the first leaders
were called "elders." This term implies seasoned or experienced Christians in the church. Because of their maturity,
wisdom, dependability, patience, and understanding of the
priorities of God's kingdom, they were selected to guide the
church. When problems arose, usually the people called for
the elders of the church to help solve them. Perceptive
churches are aware of the strength of older people in leadership
and usually provide opportunity for them to serve.

Most of the churches I have known appreciate older men
serving as deacons in the church. Some of the best friends
I had as a young minister were older deacons, who gave me
wise counsel. They showed patience and understanding with
a young preacher. For over twenty years as a seminary professor I had occasion to counsel with young ministers about their
churches. Almost all of them discovered that the strongest
leaders in their churches were older deacons. It is true that
these older men sometimes became problems because they
resisted change and discouraged young preachers in the new
ventures they proposed for the churches. In the main, however,
they were the best followers and supporters the young
preachers had. It was always good to hear from an older person,
"Preacher, I'm praying for you."

People who have lived with the Bible through the years

have a great love for it. The most faithful members of Sunday
Schools today in many of our churches are senior adults. I
teach the Businessmen's Bible Class of seventy-five men, most
of whom are over sixty-five years of age. Some of them are
in their eighties and nineties. Our attendance averages above
50 percent of the enrollment. And when one considers that
many of those enrolled are homebound and infirm and unable
to attend, the faithfulness of these older men is evident. Their
class seems to be typical of older Sunday School classes.

In our church a senior adult teacher was honored recently
by her department for forty years of teaching Junior girls.
Many other instances of older teachers could be cited. Older
adults who have remained flexible and open and loving are
accepted and appreciated by all ages, from the nursery to
the senior adult classes. The education program of the churches
will find some great assets among the older members.

Good and Faithful Stewards

The parable of the talents is one of Jesus' most famous
parables. When the steward to whom the businessman had
given five talents returned the talents with five talents more,
which he had earned, his master said, "Well done, good and
faithful servant; you have been faithful over a little, I will
set you over much; enter into the joy of your master" (Matt.
20:21).

Stewardship is a broad term which includes all of life—
talents, time, money, and influence. Dedicated Christians realize that all of life is holy and belongs to God. Many of the
most faithful stewards are older people in the church.

Recently our church took a personal inventory of our membership. It was a part of our stewardship campaign in which
we also asked our people to sign pledge cards for the budget.
The personal inventory sheet sought to find out people's talents

and their willingness to invest them. They were asked to share what they had done, what they are now doing, and what they would be willing to do in the various parts of our church program—Sunday School leadership and teaching, music department, Woman's Missionary Union, Men's Brotherhood, ministry to the homebound, community social ministries, and other specialized areas of ministry calling for the commitment of time and energy. Large numbers of the senior adults of our church responded with seriousness of purpose and joy. In many of the mission action groups of our church older persons are predominant.

Numerous older adults have been faithful stewards of their material possessions for many years. A larger percentage of them are tithers than is true of any other age group. Retired persons, who have been blessed of God financially, are among the best supporters of the church budget. Also, many provide for the church through trusts and wills.

Recently, I was inspired by a dedicated steward. Eighty-four and homebound, she had been unable to come to church for two or three years. As I was preparing to leave, she asked, "Are you going to church from here? Would you mind taking this envelope? It has my tithe in it. I can't give as much as I used to, but I want to support my church as long as I live." She had been a tither for over forty years. Her husband, who had recently died, had also been a faithful supporter of the church. She said, "When we married, he was not a tither, and I did not nag him about it. But before we had been married a year, he said, 'I want to join you in tithing our income.' "

Evangelism and the Elderly

There is great rejoicing in the church when older people accept Christ as Savior and Lord. Recently, a man about seventy-five invited me to go with him to visit a friend about the same age who had never made a confession of faith in Christ. The man's health had begun to fail, and he showed a concern about his relationship to God.

Together, we visited the man and his wife in their home. Once a successful businessman, he was now retired. His father had been a Baptist pastor in North Carolina. He said he loved his father and appreciated the work he did, but had neglected to follow his teachings in becoming a Christian and a church member. Now he wanted to know how to accomplish this. It was our privilege to witness to him and to assure him that God is always ready to welcome the believer into his kingdom.

In a few weeks this friend united with our church for baptism, and his wife, once a member of a small church in Virginia that had long since disbanded, joined by statement. One Sunday morning, as the man rose from the baptismal water, he said quietly to the pastor, "My father is smiling on me from heaven today." He is now homebound most of the time and is rarely able to come to church. Later as I visited in his home, he said, "Dr. Segler, I am now not afraid to die. When the Lord is ready for me, I am ready to go. I am happy I have made this decision."

Too often we assume that all older people have become Christians, or else they are too far along the road to respond to our witness. During 1972 the churches of the Southern Baptist Convention reported baptisms of about 8,000 persons over sixty-five years of age. There is need for evangelism of the elderly. We cannot assume that all of them are religious or have settled their relationship with God. Many of them need help. Not all senior citizens are saints. Those who are already Christians need nurturing in the Christian faith.

Older persons may be faithful witnesses in the church's program of evangelism. Many of them are happy to share their experiences with unsaved persons. Their witness is not necessarily limited to those their own age. My own mother was consistently a faithful evangelist. She instructed her eight children in the faith and influenced them to accept Christ at an early age. As the grandchildren came along, she began to pray for them and witness to them. One summer two grandchildren came to visit. While they were there, her church had a revival meeting. She took them to the services and engaged them in conversation about their relationship to the Lord. Both of them made confessions of faith and went back to their own churches to become active members. A radiant joy lighted up the face of this grandmother as she shared the experience with other persons.

Older people can team up with younger members of the church in visitation-evangelism. Past experiences in witnessing provide them with a wisdom which can be shared with less experienced persons. Others may be inspired by hearing them tell of their experiences in witnessing. One does not lose his zeal for witnessing simply because he has grown older. When the great evangelist, George Whitefield, was told his life would soon come to an end, he cried from his deathbed, "But who will preach Jesus to the people?" Of course, God had others to share in telling the good news, but the elderly preacher with a heart of compassion still yearned to see others come to Christ.

Church and Community Cooperation

The church does not live in a vacuum. Its ministry is not limited to the walls of the church building nor to the membership of the church. It is one among other institutions that serve as part of a community team in providing various health support systems for older persons. Leaders of the church should take the initiative in becoming acquainted with other community organizations and in cultivating a working relationship.

When I visited Mrs. Margaret Alston and her invalid daughter, I discovered that their only income was Social Security, which Mrs. Alston drew, and a small annuity from her deceased husband's pension. This was really not enough for an eighty year-old mother and a daughter who had been invalid and unable to work for nearly twenty years. A request to the state welfare office received an immediate response, and soon the daughter was receiving help she deserved.

Other community agencies with which the church can work include family health services, traveler's aid, the nursing association, legal counsel, medical doctors, private counselors, psychiatrists, hospitals, nursing homes, and many others. The church and other community institutions will be mutually strengthened when they work together as a team.

The church can participate in continuing education programs involving a ministry to older persons. Our church is involved in a field education program, in cooperation with Southwestern Baptist Seminary, in the education and training of seminary students. Each semester students are assigned to work with staff members in their particular areas of ministry. This semester four seminary students are helping me in a ministry to homebound persons. I supervise them according to the seminary's suggested procedures, meet them in interpersonal relations sessions, and receive from them research studies concerning needs of older persons who are homebound, either in nursing homes or in their own private homes.

Numerous colleges offer courses in geriatrics, providing training for students wanting to be involved in direct ministry to older persons. The church can work with colleges in this training, while at the same time providing a personal ministry for many elderly people who receive far too few visits. This kind of work is stimulating for both the students involved and church leaders.

Churches can use their influence in civic and political affairs to bring about better conditions for older persons generally. They should not become political action groups as such, but encourage individual members to take active part. Public servants and political leaders quite often receive moral and spiritual motivation and encouragement from the church in bringing about better legislation and political action which will benefit senior citizens.

Local churches can participate in denominational programs for the development of better ministries for older persons. Preretirement and postretirement conferences will help retirees, as well as church leaders, find ways of making life more meaningful and fulfilling for older persons. Every church should have a learning center which includes materials for the whole family. Most church libraries provide a children's section and a youth section. Why not a senior-adult section including materials in extra large print, cassettes, pamphlets, filmstrips, periodicals on aging, and other reading materials which deal with problems faced by senior adults? Denominational agencies can offer guidance and perhaps financial aid in providing these materials.

Retired persons from various occupations can combine their resources of experience—financial, legal, medical, educational, theological, and psychological wisdom—which may become invaluable to younger members of the community. The church could serve as a community catalyst in bringing this about. Church members should be encouraged to be active in retirement organizations, such as the American Association for Retired Persons, National Retired Teachers Association, and others.

4 Retirement To, Not From

When a man reaches fifty or so, he begins to meet his "noonday devil," according to Alfons Deeken.[1] Every aspect of his life seems to become a problem—his family life, his professional life, his relation to his fellowman, his sexual life. He sees the first external signs of the crisis of aging. He feels, "Perhaps I am losing my station, my usefulness, and I know I am losing my grip. My confidence is slipping. Shadows seem to be closing in on me. How can I cope with it?"

Retirement, Trauma or Triumph?

About two years before time for me to retire, I suddenly became aware that my sixty-fifth birthday was approaching. Could I face it? Was I ready to retire? No, I was not! Intellectually, I knew it was a reality. Emotionally, I was not prepared to accept it. The following are some of the problems I had to face.

I stood in the middle of my 3,000 volume library and realized I had to part with many of my books. As a minister and teacher this had been my life for forty years. My books had been my friends. I would miss them.

I thought of the classroom—the courses I had developed and taught in the seminary for twenty-one years. My life had been intermingled with all the materials I had shared with students.

I remembered that each year I had the privilege of making acquaintance with new students and having fellowship with them, of receiving their challenge to be flexible and open to change and growth. Soon I must relinquish this privilege.

There had been the comradeship of many colleagues on the faculty, some of the best persons I had ever known, and among them intimate friendships. To a great extent that fellowship would be limited, to say the least.

Then there was the routine of my work. It was structured for me. It made me feel secure. I had become something of a "workaholic." Could I give that up? Could I find new and creative ways of planning and pursuing my vocation?

I was concerned about opportunities for further ministry. What kind of job can I find? Will I be needed? Can I find satisfaction in what I will be doing? Will I be able to continue my writing?

I must consider future housing and living conditions. How long can Fannie Mae and I maintain our home? As grandparents, we would like to continue to live on the old home place where our children and grandchildren can return for visits.

Then there is the future economic situation. Can our style of life be maintained? Will Social Security and minister's retirement monthly check from the Annuity Board be sufficient?

Can my wife and I adjust to our new relationship in the home? Can she stand more of me? Can we sustain and even enrich our companionship?

One begins to think about how he will spend his last days. Will I have adequate care? Will I be isolated? Will family and friends remember me?

Death comes in old age. There will not be too many years

left. Can I face up to my own death? How does one prepare for the end of this pilgrimage?

These are the kinds of questions I had to face. Doubtless, they are very much like the questions all people facing retirement must encounter. All of us need help in finding answers. Intellectually, we must acquire factual knowledge. Emotionally, we must learn to accept the reality of change, to cope with it, and to make whatever adjustments are necessary for meaningful living.

As I struggled through these questions, and meditated upon the meaning of life thus far, I was able to make certain affirmations concerning retirement.

God gives us the ability to change, to adjust. There is a certain resilience built into the very structure of life.

I can walk by faith. Life has always been an adventure of faith. Actually, up to this point I have not been able to walk entirely by sight.

I believe I can count on family ties' being strong enough to hold. I shall not be walking alone but living in the strength of commitments made across the years. Loved ones will share the evening of life with me.

I believe in our social order. Our American people will find ways of caring for life at every stage. We shall continually search for better ways of making life meaningful for the aging person.

I believe my church is the kind of fellowship that will remember me and include me among its many older members.

I believe God has ministers who will minister to me. Some of them are laymen, fellow-Christians I have known across the years.

God loves me. He has proved it. Life has been full of blessings. He will not forget nor forsake me now. Life is his gift on to the end.

I can and do affirm life—with God, his people, his world, his kingdom!

Facing Up to Reality

"I like things the way they are. I don't like to change so often. The world is moving too fast. I like the feeling of being settled. Change is really disturbing to me." How often such statements come from persons in the middle and older years. We must face the reality that life is not static; it is constantly moving. We, too, are always changing whether we are aware of it or not.

Retirement and old age must be accepted. As life moves along, we have to give up some things and accept some other things which we may not like. We can learn to accept these things with serenity without leaving off significant activities. Let us remain as active, as sociable and friendly as we can, despite an unavoidable measure of loneliness and separation. Resisting the aging process is unrealistic; it is a losing fight. Learning to age successfully can bring victory and even joy.

Recently, a personal experience brought this thought home to my wife and me. Fannie Mae and I were invited to the hundred-and-ninth anniversary celebration of the First Baptist Church, Garland, Texas, where I was pastor twenty-nine years ago. About ten o'clock that Sunday morning I drove under the portico alongside the beautiful sanctuary, let my companion out, and went to park the car while she waited for me.

When the day was over, she shared some intimate reveries with me. As she stood at the entrance of the large sanctuary, built years after we left there, she asked herself, "What was here on this spot twenty-nine years ago? Why, this was the front porch of the old parsonage!" Then she remembered the days when our three children were small. She imagined sitting in the porch swing telling them stories or watching them crawl around on the lawn under the shade of the large trees. Now all of this is gone. And the children are gone. Dana is now thirty-five, Sam thirty-one, and Sylvia twenty-nine. They are all married and living in Corpus Christi, Texas, Geneva, Switzerland, and Austin, Texas, respectively. And we have five grandchildren!

All of a sudden this mother and grandmother asked, "And where am I in the midst of this change and in the time sequence of it all? A sort of eerie feeling, and much nostalgia swept over me." But she soon came back to the present and realized she would not change any of it, even if she could. She was grateful for the ongoingness of life, and is looking forward to the so-called "retirement" years with anticipation.

It is good to be able to acknowledge change and welcome it without being overcome with its mystery, its losses, its demands, and its inevitability. It also has its compensations.

Preparation for Retirement

Obviously, one must prepare for any change that takes place in his life. The extent of the preparation will determine the success with which he accepts the change when it comes. When does one begin preparing for retirement? Actually, all of life that has gone before furnishes the foundation on which life is built from this point on. However, there is a sense in which specific education for retirement can take place. It involves intellectual understanding, emotional acceptance, and inner or spiritual commitment to a purposeful future.

The "change process" necessitates a willingness to set priorities. Two things are essential: accurate information about things that will change our lives, and the development of problem-solving skills for coping with change.

Preparation for retirement programs, used by many organizations and individuals, includes a classic change model outlined in four stages:

Awareness of retirement problems and the consequences one may expect from a given plan is essential. Also, the individual must be aware of the attitudes and hopes for retirement he brings with him on the pilgrimage.

One must analyze the problems of aging and retirement and explore the various resources, solutions, and plans worthy of consideration.

Furthermore, *a plan of action* on programs and procedures for retirement must be adopted and pursued. Knowledge obtained will be used in developing skills, making decisions, and solving problems.

Finally, *actualization* toward internalizing expectations and developing the capacity for self-renewal must be a reality for the individual. Inner resources must be appropriated in order to actualize one's philosophy of the closing phases of life.

In American society sixty-five is the usual mandatory retirement age, and there does not seem to be any prospect of changing that soon. In fact, there is a trend toward an earlier retirement. A rapidly growing number of middle-aged people are seeking to relinquish some of the pressures of full-time work and to find ways of enjoying their work before it comes to an end.

In a recent seminar in Washington, D.C., an administration analyst recommended that every individual, where possible, participate in two or three different kinds of work during his lifetime. His idea of vocation: "multiservice goals" for everyone. Thus, when one comes to retirement, he moves to a plane of activity which may quite legitimately call for less energy, and at the same time match the inner desires he has for self-fulfillment.

Some students of gerontology suggest that it may be helpful

to view retirement years in three stages or phases: a fun phase, a phase of protected living, and a phase of withdrawal or disengagement.[2]

The *"fun" phase* is that period in which persons are still vigorous and have time to engage in enjoyable things they have wanted to do. This period lasts about ten years during which time health and financial resources are adequate to permit enjoyment in a variety of activities. Those who take early retirement will have more years for this fun phase.

The *phase of protected living* may be precipitated when health conditions begin to limit physical activity. It may also be hastened by the death of a spouse. Further, with the decreasing number of old friends, the aging person begins to look for protected living, perhaps in retirement centers where there is greater physical security, more conveniences, and available medical care. The majority of people at this age continue to live in their own homes or apartments, but are less involved in community activity and social life. Others move in with their children. A smaller number move into retirement homes or communities.

The *final phase of withdrawal or disengagement* often comes with the loss of a spouse, the beginning of ill health, the loss of many old friends, or rejection by children. During this period, older persons have great need for support and help from others—shelter, personal care, and medical attention. In a later chapter this phase will be discussed in greater detail.

As has been pointed out before, the retirement years are related to the whole life cycle. One's philosophy of life and perspective on life as a whole can help to set the retirement years in proper focus.

It is generally agreed that the life cycle has three major components. The first component emphasizes study and preparation for a career. The second places primary emphasis on productive work. It also should include continuing education, assisting individuals in building the capacity for self-renewal throughout life, and education for continuing productivity in various ways. The third phase places the emphasis upon the wisdom of experience, self-fulfillment in achieving goals for life enrichment, which limitations of time have hindered thus far, and ministry to persons in the community, wherever one's talents are most needed.

Simplification, Not Disengagement

When Turner Catledge, former executive editor and vice-president of the *New York Times*, retired May 1, 1970, he said his greatest problem was subjective in character. Brought up on the Puritan ethic of useful, lifelong, productive labor, like many other Americans, he felt compulsive about work and became uneasy when he left the routine of productive activity. This attitude often becomes an irritant in the life of the retiree.

I, personally, have to plead guilty to being a "workaholic." It is difficult to slow down when one has spent all his life working hard in the belief that he must always produce that which is visible and measurable.

I discovered this one day recently while working in our garden. Reared on the farm, I always worked hard and tried to set goals of measurable, physical achievement. One hot summer afternoon, at sixty-five I was spading around a peach tree when I realized that my heart was pounding. I was really straining at my work. I was furiously beating the clods as if I had only a short time to complete the task. I paused, amused at my stupidity. The next forkful of dirt was turned at a little slower pace, and soon I was relaxing and enjoying my favorite hobby.

Wayne Oates, formerly professor of psychology of religion

at Southern Baptist Theological Seminary, presented me with a real challenge in his *Confessions of a Workaholic.*[3] Having confessed that he was a workaholic, he characterized the life of such an addict, showing how it affects his family, his associates, and his own state of mind. He particularly showed its effects upon the personal religion of the addict himself.

Oates then offered hope for remaking the life of the workaholic. The essence of this hope rests in the conviction that life is worth living and that a person's life can be made better, can actually be remade. Life does not have to end in futility. A radical change can take place. It probably will involve suffering. Like withdrawal from addiction to drugs, the process of changing one's outlook on work is painful. This kind of change often has to take place in the life of a retiree. There must be a real conversion. Based upon the grace of God, a new affirmation of life where it is can bring God's blessings in abundance.

The retiree will have to recondition his work habits and accept his new assignment as a sublimation of his need to work. Deciding to change one's routine and the pace of his activities calls for the same kind of commitment he has known before in his vocation. Life as a retiree is still vocation as God's gift.

Retirement years offer a challenge for continued growth and development. They should not be years of deterioration and regression but a challenge to pursue worthwhile goals in a different manner. Dr. Abraham Heschel, in an address to the White House Conference on Aging in 1961, warned against the "trivialization of life" in the retirement years. Worthwhile objectives should be adopted and pursued. For example, recreation and hobbies are necessary and can contribute to the enjoyment of life. However, preoccupation with games and hobbies can eliminate boredom only temporarily. An overem-

phasis on recreation can lead to "a pickled existence, preserved
in brine with spices."

Dr. Heschel said that recreation should not serve as a substitute for work one has done in earlier years. On the other hand,
it must not be allowed to bring back the trivialization of
existence. One ought to enter retirement years in the manner
he enters the senior year at a university, in exciting anticipation
of consummation. He no longer feels competitive with his
fellowman. What the nation needs, according to Dr. Heschel,
is senior universities, universities for the aged where wise men
teach the potentially wise, where the purpose of learning is
not a career for material productivity, but for the sake of
learning itself.

Learning the art of leisure is another part of preparation
for retirement living. Leisure is a good and glorious gift as
a change from the routine of work. However, there is danger
in losing the rhythm and pace of work when you really have
time on your hands. The only way to handle it is by means
of self-discipline. It has to be combatted daily by calling up
inner reserves.

For example, now that I am retired from the routine, hourly
schedule of classroom teaching, faculty meetings, and commit-
tee work, I am "on my own." I cannot depend upon an author-
ity figure or organizational structure for my schedule.

For example, I am still involved in writing, which has always
been one of my major interests. But this book has been one
of my most difficult assignments. It is not the subject, for I
am deeply interested it it. It is the situation—retirement and
leisure, learning to handle time. Writing is hard work. One
free lance writer said writing was for her a "painful experience,
much worse than having a baby." She was the mother of three.
The birth pains of producing a new book, especially in the
retirement years, seem to be greater than ever.

Keeping busy in retirement is important, but it is human nature to become lazy in body and mind. So, friend, beware of the leisure of retirement. Keep your mind and body active by self-discipline, the exercise of strong willpower, purposeful prayer, meditation, and action. Especially action! One never completes what is never begun. He must move toward the objective. Now, I must remind myself again that, of all the professions, perhaps writing makes the biggest demand on one's self-discipline. Leisure time is a good servant but a poor master.

Retirement and the Home

It takes two to retire successfully. Husband and wife must plan and practice it together. He does not have to become a problem around the house, always under foot. One woman said, "I can never get my housework done with him around. First he was a guest; now he is a nuisance."

According to Peterson, retirement must be recognized as a crisis. The end of a work career brings with it a number of role shocks. One of the most severe is the readjustment of the relationship of husband and wife, who have become accustomed to seeing each other only a limited number of hours each day. Now, when partners are forced into continuous closeness and confrontation, misery can result.

This can be a growth period for both spouses. Just as they went through an adjustment period in the early years of marriage, learning things about each other and adjusting to each other's personality, this can also be a time of learning still more about each other. There are mysteries about individual personhood which can never be fully fathomed. New qualities may be discovered which will enrich the lives of both partners.

Why not try role swapping part of the time? At least, he can take on some of the chores traditionally known as woman's work. She can perhaps become interested in some of his outside activities which both of them can enjoy together.

Men have found the following rules useful in helping their wives also retire. Take an inventory of things that need fixing and proceed to fix them—painting, upholstering, patching, and so forth. Take on certain chores in housekeeping, such as scrubbing floors and cleaning the bath. She will gladly relinquish these. Learn to help with the grocery shopping. Designate for yourself a permanent work space, other than the living room area. Cook breakfast occasionally, or regularly, as she desires. Allow her freedom of space and activity to which she is accustomed.

Travel, make plans together to see places you have longed to explore—New England fall foliage, Florida Everglades, Mississippi gardens, Texas piney woods, the green, quiet Texas hill country, or the snowcapped Canadian Rockies. Get involved as a team in community volunteer services—hospitals, low-income community ministries, retarded children, ministry to the homebound and elderly.

Upon retirement, one man came home and said to his wife, "Now we are right back where we started. The children are gone, and you and I have to start life all over again together." In a sense, this is true.

The retirement years will bring either enrichment and enjoyment to life or deterioration and misery. It all depends upon the resolutions of both husband and wife. Persons who have prepared well and who have anticipated this period of life will be better able to adjust. The disorganizing aspects of the crisis will be less serious if couples are intellectually and psychologically prepared ahead of time, according to gerontologists Donahue, Aubach, and Pollock.[4]

This is a good time for the renewal of marital vows. In the beginning of marriage, each partner makes a commitment to the other, in the hope that each can contribute something in making life mutually more enjoyable. The commitment of self includes total personhood—physical, mental, emotional, and spiritual. One's companion is a gift from God. Why not make these retirement years a time for thanksgiving and celebration and a new commitment to make the last of life the very best.

Tournier says that in order to understand each other, we need to grasp the importance of the past.[5] Reviewing the past by sharing thoughts and feelings can deepen marriage at this stage. If we hope to understand each other, we must listen long, with great interest, and without prejudice. Discovering what is deepest in each other is a movement we begin in marriage and develop continuously throughout life.

Complete honesty brings about deeper understanding. This kind of open dialogue in the later years of marriage includes a kind of confession. The experience should be reciprocal, a courageous confession calling forth comparable response from one's partner. Thus, facing life together, moments in God's presence, full of truth, love, and mutual respect, can bring a sort of second movement of souls into marital oneness.

Tournier concludes, "Because of such moments we have come to experience much more than a wonderful marriage; we have come, through each other, to experience God himself."

Simplification—Stewardship of Material Things

Our ability to accept the simplification of life and to relinquish some of the things which have been such an important part of our lives will depend upon our concept of stewardship. A certain amount of money is essential to sustain life, but it is not the major support of life, and it ought not be the supreme concern of life.

Dr. James Knight, Dean of Tulane Medical School, trained

in medicine and theology, warns against perverted motives in acquiring and using money. He says one may view material possessions as a symbol of power to be used in dominating other people—the family, the community, the nation. The possessor becomes the possessed. He loses the primacy of the personal, and the qualities of love, mercy, and generosity are perverted into ruthlessness, miserliness, and loneliness.

Remember Jesus' challenge, "Do not lay up for yourselves treasures on the earth . . . but lay up treasures in heaven" where eternal values are never corroded away. He said, "Seek first the kingdom of God and his righteousness, and all these things will be yours as well" (Matt. 6:33). Let us go back to the Model Prayer and trust our Father to give us today the bread we need (Matt. 6:9-15).

Mrs. Paul, eighty-eight, willed her home and furniture to her favorite school. Reflecting upon her action she said, "I enjoyed all those beautiful things for years. I don't need them anymore. Let some younger people now enjoy them."

Free to Serve

One of life's highest goals is that of becoming a servant. Every normal person would like to serve his fellowman, to make a contribution to society. Dr. Ethel Percy Andrus, founder of the American Association of Retired Persons and National Retired Teachers' Association, enunciated the theme: "To serve, not to be served." She went on to say that it is only in the giving of one's self to others that we truly live.

Most older persons remember saying in the years before retirement, "I would like to serve there and there, if I only had the time." Now we have more time, and the opportunities were never greater than today. Old age was never intended to be a state of "living deadness," but rather a maturing into another, purposeful life. The retirement years provide the opportunity to live a full life by investing life for others.

Volunteer services are becoming one of the major means of providing human services in America. E. C. Lindeman says the health of a democratic society may be measured in terms of the quality of services rendered by citizens who act in "obedience to the unenforceable." [6]

Serving others brings satisfaction in personal growth and development. The individual needs to volunteer as much as the community needs him. In ministering to others, the search for personal meaning, identity, self-renewal, and interpersonal relationships are built toward fulfillment.

In our postindustrial economy, the trend is toward human-service jobs rather than thing-production jobs. It is projected that soon 75 percent of the work roles in our society will be in human service. Volunteer service functions in the community include recreation and leisure time, culture and education, economics, politics, welfare, religion, health, social control, mass communication, and many others.

There is a challenge for the older segment of our population to become involved in volunteer services, considering the number of us and the resources we have to offer. Dedicated older persons will find self-actualization possible in volunteer services. Many feel this is the opportunity for the repayment of a "service received" debt.

Recently, I witnessed two examples of selfless service. In one of our hospitals, as I approached the desk at the entrance of the intensive care unit, I saw a gray-haired lady, a member of our church, serving the public by acting as a volunteer receptionist. With a smile, she gave the information I desired.

Then, as I visited a nonambulatory patient in a nursing home, I encountered another bright spirit. She said, "When I entered the nursing home eight years ago, I was able to get around and minister to many of the older people here.

I had a ball! Now, I have to depend on someone to help me." She served others as long as she had the strength, and then became the grateful recipient of ministries others offered to her. I recalled the words of Jesus: "Whoever among you wants to be great must become the servant of all—just as the Son of Man has not come to be served but to serve, and to give his life to set many others free" (Matt. 20:27-28, Phillips).

5 *I Go Not Gentle*

Do not go gentle into that good night,
Old age should burn and rave at close of day;

Older persons identify easily with these lines by Dylan
Thomas. We all want to remain active as long as possible.
No person wants to be cut off from his life of usefulness. Much
less does he want to be cast off from his human community.
It can happen very easily.

Recently, I saw a ninety-minute teleplay on the CBS *Play-
house* series entitled "Do Not Go Gentle into That Good
Night." The plot centered on Peter Schermann, a strong man
who had been shaken and saddened by his wife's death. He
had become an unwanted guest in his own home, now occupied
by his selfish forty-five-year-old son, his whining wife, and their
children. Lost and lonely, Peter, past three-score-years-and-ten,
permitted his children to send him to an "old folks" home,
full of the senile, the ailing, and the defeated, all being treated
like irresponsible children. He soon stormed out of that place
and went to another institution which had recreation programs
and workshops. Here his old interest in his craft of cabi-
net-making was revived.

Gradually Peter's strength returned, and he marched back

to his own house determined to pick up the threads of life in the real world again. Peter announced positively to his family that he was still head of his house. "Happiness comes from work!" exclaimed Schermann in his rebellion.

This play did not present the whole truth about aging, since it omitted that transition period when older persons must disengage from intensive activity and learn how to carve out for themselves a new kind of life experience, perhaps at a slower pace.

Furthermore, not all nursing homes are filled with people cast off by their families merely to wait for the death angel. One nursing home director has expressed the ideal which all of us in present-day society want for our older citizens. He speaks of "the good life, a way of life, the quality of life, adding depth as well as length to life." He said further, "Our home is not only a place where older people come to live, but come to life. We see our mission as one that not only adds years to life, but life to those years."

In My Own Home

The majority of older people in America still live at home. It is not unusual to see married couples celebrating their fiftieth and sixtieth wedding anniversaries. One of them, or perhaps both of them, have enough health and strength to maintain the home independently.

Many of them are living alone, having lost the spouse by death. Generally, the wife lives longer than the husband. Consequently, she is now left to face life with a new challenge and perspective.

There are also great numbers of older persons who have never married. These single individuals come to retirement and old age with a spirit of independence and courage. These, as well as widows, will often seek someone to live in with them, perhaps a relative, a close friend, or a colleague. It is my privilege to visit regularly in the home of two sisters, both widowed, one of whom is ridden with arthritis so seriously she is unable to care for all her needs. Her sister, slightly younger, shares her strength with her.

Many older people have adult children living with them, while others live in the homes of their children or other relatives. Most families in our culture make all possible efforts to take care of their aged relatives at home.

Because of deteriorating physical and/or mental abilities, safety precautions should be taken in the home to protect elderly persons against health hazards. The following safety measures may be followed: well-lighted stairways with handrails, non-skid carpets and rugs, grab bars, rubber mats and seats in the bathtub, night lights to prevent falling or stumbling, easily accessible storage areas to eliminate stepladders, tripod canes offering firm support, ramps for entering or leaving the house, lightweight cooking utensils with insulated handles, and chairs and beds adjusted so that feet will be flat on the floor in the sitting position.

Some communities offer a variety of noninstitutional services that enable older persons to maintain their own homes: friendly visitors, telephone reassurance, "meals on wheels," and various home clinical and therapeutic services.

Most people over sixty-five live in familiar surroundings. About 80 percent head their own households, roughly one-half live with their spouses, about 18 percent reside with other persons, either relatives or non-relatives, approximately 5 percent live in homes for the aging, and slightly over 1 percent are in mental and other institutions. About one-third of them live in dilapidated housing, and 45 percent receiving Social Security payments are in need of better housing accommodations.

Making the Transition

Mrs. Howard stayed in her own home as long as possible. When she started having "blackouts" and falling, her doctor recommended that she go where she could have continuous nursing care. She thought about it for several months. During this time she discussed with me the possibility of moving into a nursing home, which I encouraged her to do. She had no member of the family to care for her, and she could not find anyone to live in with her. Finally, she decided it was the sensible thing.

After the transition to the nursing home, she said to me, "One of the hardest things was leaving my own kitchen and all the pots and pans I had used through the years. But things are not as important as persons." She concluded, "It's not like being home, but I have no complaints. I am comfortable and am making friends with many of the people here."

The decision to move from one's own home to a nursing home calls for thorough consideration. It may involve all members of the family and perhaps professional people whose counsel can be helpful.

Dr. William Poe suggests the following questions should help reach the decision: Is the person too heavy, too disabled, or too depressed to be adequately nursed at home? Is the home too crowded to have an invalid occupying space needed for other members of the family? Can the older person have adequate nursing, either by someone living in the home or by outside help? Can the patient be left alone, or must someone watch him at all times, lest he wander away? Is needed medical attention more readily available in the nursing home? Which is more feasible economically, extra help at home or the expense of a nursing home? [1]

An important factor is that the older person himself must

participate in the decision to enter a nursing home. Mr. John Dale's wife had recently died. Now past eighty, he experienced frequent periods of depression. Family members decided to move him into a nursing home.

About a week after he entered the home, I found him angry and rebellious. "I don't know why I'm here," he said. "I feel like I am in a prison. They won't let me get out and walk around. I don't have enough room here. See how small this closet is. When my family asked me to sign some papers to come here, I thought it was for a temporary stay. Now I feel trapped. I don't see why I can't go back to my own home. I don't know what will happen to it or to my car."

I reasoned with him that he could no longer care for himself in his own home. His family had observed this carefully. They were not prepared to give him the care he needed. I assured him the staff of the nursing home would give him good care and encouraged him to make friends with other residents. Fortunately, he had an excellent roommate whose outlook on life was positive and hopeful.

Doubtless, Mr. Dale's family could have prepared him psychologically for making the move, but they may have felt some guilt in making the decision. Perhaps a little patience and a clear understanding would have helped him accept it with a good attitude. He is now handling his grief better than he did for a while, and he is making friends who help him cope with his disappointment and resentment.

Choosing a Nursing Home

Families can find find help in locating appropriate nursing homes. The city health department, responsible for licensing and inspection, can furnish a list of facilities. Physicians, family service agencies, church groups, and senior citizens' organizations can help to evaluate various homes.

Several nursing homes should be visited before the choice is made. One trained sociologist suggests the following points be kept in mind during the visit: How are you received? Is information given freely or is the atmosphere guarded? Are staff and residents friendly? Are they easy to talk with? Is the home crowded? Noisy? Attractively furnished? Does it have pleasant grounds?

Physical arrangements are important. Notice carefully the private rooms; estimate space when more than one person shares a room; check on bath facilities, the communal dining room, lounges, recreation areas, adequate clothing storage, easy access by wheelchairs, grab rails.

Nursing homes certainly should be clean and free of odors. The rooms should be properly cared for. Adequate laundry arrangements are absolutely essential. Rooms may be made more comfortable and attractive if residents bring some of their own furnishings.

Many nursing homes have programs for social activities. They often have a large center where people can gather for occasions of interest to the entire community—entertainment, recreation, group discussions, religious services, and so forth. Homes that have activity directors usually provide a well-rounded program for the residents.

Food services are high on the priority list. A trained dietitian can prepare meals suitable for older people. Special diets and training in self-feeding are important parts of health programs for residents.

An adequate staff is often difficult to maintain, particularly on the limited budgets of nursing homes. A reasonably adequate staff should care for medical, dental, nursing, barber and beauty aids, rehabilitation in physical, hearing, and speech therapy, help in dressing and bathing, toilet and bladder training, and so forth.

Financial arrangements must be made clear to the new resident and those responsible for admitting him. Some nursing homes accept only those persons who can pay directly for their services. Others admit persons on Medicare and Medicaid programs. Often these programs include state welfare aid for those below the poverty level. All of these economic policies should be thoroughly understood before a choice is finally made.

There are various levels of care provided by nursing homes. The Health, Education and Welfare Department recognizes two levels of care—intermediate and skilled. In some states intermediate care is further broken down into two levels, Intermediate Care II, or custodial care, which includes supervision of personal needs and adjustments to institutional living, but not complex nursing care; and Intermediate Care III, on a day-to-day basis, which requires skilled nursing techniques and/or medical therapy. For skilled care, a registered nurse is responsible for the total nursing service.

Needs of the Homebound

The terms "homebound" or "shut-in" are relative terms. They usually mean persons confined most of the time, unable to get out and participate in the ongoing activities of society as they once did. With help, many are able to go to the doctor's office, attend church services, go on errands, participate in some social activity, or simply take a ride as a means of diversion.

The psychological needs of the homebound must be considered. Perhaps the most universal problem of the homebound person is *loneliness*. After hundreds of visits with elderly persons and in field education with many seminary students working with the homebound, I have observed that loneliness is the number one problem. Every human being needs the love of a caring person or persons. When one is isolated, his loneliness is intensified. Every one of us identifies with the psalmist: "Cast me not off in the time of old age; forsake me not when my strength faileth" (Psalm 71:9).

Loneliness is everybody's problem. It afflicts all of us—married or single, young or old, sick or well—none totally escapes it. How shall we cope with it? Give in and feel sorry for ourselves? Withdraw into isolation? We need not. In the first place, we must realize there is a large space in the inner being which calls for relationship, the need for other persons. Augustine acknowledged the theology of loneliness: "Thou hast made us for thyself, O God, and our souls are restless until they find their rest in thee." Thank God for this part of my being that feels the need for other persons. We should neither deny it nor feel ashamed of it.

We can do something about our own loneliness and that of others. We can make ourselves available to others, keep up communication with our fellowman, and reach out to develop new relationships, a new community of persons.

One woman, confined to her home, handled her own loneliness by keeping in touch with other persons by telephone. She regularly called her friends in nursing homes to try to cheer them up.

Fear and *anxiety* are also a constant problem for the homebound: fear of sickness, anxiety about financial security, fear of the loss of loved ones and friends, anxiety about the future, and fear of death.

Anxiety can be negative, or it can be positive. Man's responsibility for making choices sets up a certain amount of anxiety within him. Where there is meaning, there is a degree of anxiety. To be anxious is to be concerned, to be interested, to care how life turns out. Anxiety makes possible exhilaration and excitement. Anxiety may be defined as a God-given ability by which we can experience concern. Normal concern is a good thing.

There are various kinds of anxiety. The *anxiety of finiteness* is a part of man's creatureliness. The greatest Christian saints have felt the distance between themselves and God, the great chasm of mystery. Then there is *environmental anxiety.* The specific situation in which I find myself, particularly when I am uprooted and face change, can produce great anxiety.

Older persons are often threatened by *economic anxiety.* Being anxious about material things can become a threatening cloud. The *anxiety of sin and guilt* is a universal experience. Sin separates us from God and creates estrangement from our fellowman, whether one is young or aged.

We can learn to live with anxiety. Determining the cause of one's anxiety in a given situation is a step toward solving it. Sometimes we need help in defining the problem, perhaps the help of a counselor or a psychiatrist. Self-discipline is essential to self-education. Accepting my finiteness as a person can give reassurance and challenge. If real guilt is the reason for anxiety, we can be reconciled to God in Christ. Faith in God may not remove all anxiety, but it helps to reduce it and keep it in proper perspective. "If we confess our sins, he is faithful and just, and will forgive our sins and cleanse us from all unrighteousness" (1 John 1:9).

Depression is one of the gravest problems older people face. If it is not handled properly, it can lead to apathy and despair. Every individual sometime faces the dark night of the soul. Many of the most gifted and creative persons have been subject to periods of depression. A list of those who have made significant contributions would include: John Bunyan, author of *Pilgrim's Progress;* Thomas á Kempis, author of *Imitation of Christ;* the prolific writers, Charles Lamb and Samuel Johnson; the gifted composer, Chopin; and the great American commoner and president, Abraham Lincoln.

No one seems to know all the causes of depression. It is a low emotional tide which the individual quite often cannot handle. It may be due to one's physical condition—low metabolism, thyroid deficiency, constipation, toxic condition due to blood infection, glandular disturbances, and so forth. Depression is not inherited from one's parents, as some suppose. Fatigue, brought on by physical and emotional activity, is often the forerunner of depression. Excessive use of alcohol and drugs can lead to despair. Grief experiences are frequently the main cause. A state of apathy may result.

My mother experienced depression in the form of apathy at about sixty years of age, following the tragic death of my younger sister. Only two years before, our stepfather had died. The shock of this additional loss was more than Mother could handle. Her reaction was a feeling of physical illness. After doctors determined she was not really physically ill, I sensed that her apathy was probably due to emotional shock. She had lost her desire to go on with the responsibilities of living. We took her to our home and nursed her back to health. When she regained her strength, she went on living victoriously. She died at the age of eighty-one, full of courage and joy right up to the end of her earthly pilgrimage.

Remember, this too will pass. Patience and faith will help us wait for the tide to rise. Wait on God. He is at work. In his *Letters From Prison* Dietrich Bonhoeffer said, "I shall like to speak of God not at the borders of life but in its center, not in weakness but in strength, not therefore in man's suffering and death but in his life and prosperity. God is the 'beyond' in the midst of our life."

An eminent psychiatrist, Dr. Leonard Cammer, has written a paperback book *Up From Depression* which may prove helpful to those facing this problem. Dr. Cammer calls attention to some of the general symptoms of depression such as sadness, sleep difficulties, poor appetite, loss of self-confidence, self-neglect, and so forth. He then outlines several means of overcoming depression: drug treatment, physical therapy, electroshock treatment, psychotherapy, and psychiatric hospitalization. He observes that the return to health is largely dependent on the family's participation in the recovery process.

The *fear of death and dying* is a common problem of older persons. A later chapter will deal with the problem of death and dying more adequately. Those who minister to the elderly should be aware of their emotional problems and seek to find ways of helping them.

The Nursing Home Resident

Frances Faunce has shared her experience as a resident of a nursing home in her book *The Nursing Home Visitor*.[2] She testifies that life in a nursing home can be both interesting and challenging; it can be a maturing experience. A positive attitude on the part of the resident can help one make the transition from one's private home to the nursing home. Expecting the good can reinforce a pleasant experience.

Preparation for the "take-off" will include business items, such as personal identification, Social Security card, and hospital insurance card. Personal articles must be selected—essential clothing properly labeled and numerous toilet articles, such as toothpaste, denture containers, brush, comb, and hair nets. Then, there are miscellaneous items—luminated clock-radio with extension cord, television (if desired), laundry bag, correspondence address book, memo pads, stationery, and pencils. Reading materials will be important—Bibles, devotional materials, and magazines. Do not overlook medical aids (as permitted), such as favorite throat lozenges, foot comforts, eye drops, and solution for contact lenses.

Miss Faunce insists that the resident understand the functions and services of the home. He should be aware that medical care (house doctor, nurses, and nurses' aides), religious ministry (ministers, musicians, church groups), and various services (cleaning women, maintenance men, hairdresser, chiropodist, physical therapist, and volunteer workers) will be available to him.

Nursing home residents often find satisfaction in performing certain chores and ministries for other residents. Using one's skills brings fulfillment to oneself and blessings to others. Things one might do: deliver mail, act as receptionist, assist with mailing materials, aid in preparing the bulletin, help plan programs and activities, as talents indicate, care for plants and birds, conduct games, read to other residents, and help them with letter writing.

The Ministry of Visitors

Frequently as I enter a room at a nursing home, the resident will brighten up and say, "I'm so glad you came! It's so lonely here." Recently, I said to our congregation, "Our homebound members need our ministry, appreciate our ministry, and deserve our ministry."

Visitors can come from all age groups—adults, retired adults, teenagers—and from all walks of life—ministers, educators, businessmen, housewives, doctors, lawyers, psychologists, psychiatrists—each offering his particular gift based upon his training, experience, and desire to share with others.

Ministries which can be performed by visitors include: (1) direct personal ministry (listening and talking, reading aloud, letter writing, manicuring, mending clothing, sewing on buttons, running shopping errands, transporting residents to musicals, the theater, the church, or the doctor's office, combing hair, shaving men); (2) conducting religious services, worship, Bible study, group singing; (3) showing movies, travelogs, and color slides; (4) helping with arts and crafts, working with your hands; (5) conducting games and recreation activities; (6) providing tea cart services with cookies, coffee, tea, or punch; (7) adopting individuals and providing a foster home ministry with occasional treats to outside activities, arranging special visits to the family home; (8) arranging car pools and bus transportation for groups to musicals and community programs.

Personal visitation is the most widely needed ministry. It is important, therefore, that we learn how to be effective in visitation. A positive attitude is essential. One should learn to be comfortable with older persons, especially the handicapped. Learning how to be at ease is important.

Human presence, "being present" to the individual, offering the total self at the specific time is the first requirement. Relationship is developed by openness, self-giving, and receiving. Intelligent listening will encourage the resident to open up and share his concerns. Silence often has great value. Sharing quiet periods may create awareness of a third Presence, God himself.

Touching can bring human warmth and acceptance—grasping a hand, placing an arm about the shoulders, or even a tender touch of the hand on a brow may have healing for the spirit.

Sharing a word, "the Word," the good news of God's love can be invaluable.[3] Sharing in prayer—waiting together before God, offering the blessing of assurance, forgiveness—can bring healing and strength.

Myron C. Madden, director of the department of pastoral care, Southern Baptist Hospital, New Orleans, Louisiana, challenges Christians to share the grace of God by serving as ministers of blessing and healing. The origin and power of all healing and blessing begins with God. He often chooses to mediate his blessing through redeemed servants. Dr. Madden says, "The Christian is a healer of broken spirits. He should be willing to lay his hands gently, yet perhaps firmly, on the tender areas of suffering, so that he might give the very strength of his life in sharing his blessing with others." [4]

Like a Bridge

I awoke with a start as my telephone rang at 2:30 A.M. A neighbor said, "Mr. Dreksel just died. Can you come? Mrs. Dreksel needs you." I thought, if anyone deserves my ministry at this hour, Mrs. Dreksel does. Mr. Dreksel, eighty-seven, had been in a nursing home for nearly a year. His death came suddenly, unexpectedly. His wife, eighty-three, had been ill and unable to visit the nursing home for five days. Her eighty-year-old sister, Miss Bertha, lived with her and needed constant care herself.

In the home that morning we talked and then read Psalm 23 and John 14:1-6 and had prayer together. Mrs. Dreksel said, "We hated to bother you in the middle of the night, but we really appreciate your coming. It has helped us." As I drove back the seven miles across the city to my home, and reflected on the experience, over the car radio came the song "Like a Bridge over Troubled Water, I Will Lay Me Down." A good feeling came over me. Back on my bed, I seemed to hear our Lord saying, "Take my hand, brother minister. For this cause you were born into the world, you were called to the ministry of shepherding." I went to sleep aware that the fellowship of Christ in a comforting ministry brings comfort to those who serve as well as to those who are served.

6 *Why Must I Be Sick?*

Following a fall, Mrs. Richards had recently become a resident of a nursing home. She complained to me that she was not making as rapid recovery as she used to. Then, with a humorous twinkle, she added, "But, then, what can I expect at the age of ninety!" I replied, "Yes, these old bodies do begin to wear out after a while, don't they?"

I suppose all of us at one time or another have asked, "Why must I be sick?" The question "why" has been asked ever since Job shared his philosophy of evil and suffering. The apostle Paul had a "thorn in the flesh" which he could not escape, although he prayed earnestly for God to remove it. Even Jesus himself, perfect man that he was, prayed in Gethsemane that he might be spared the cup of suffering he was facing, and on the cross he agonized, "My God, why hast thou forsaken me?"

We are always in the process of dying and being born again. We begin to die as soon as we are born, and we struggle to overcome the sicknesses which point toward death. We are experiencing death in the midst of life, as well as life in the face of death.

Longfellow reminded us,

Thy fate is the fate of all,

Into each life some rain must fall,
Some days must be dark and dreary.

Therefore, in our time, we are not likely to escape sickness
and suffering in our struggle to become whole persons. We
can, however, learn the art of preventive health and the secret
of coping victoriously with our sicknesses.

I had my first serious illness when I was fifty-six years of
age. I had never before been in a hospital as a patient. During
a record snowstorm in 1964 I shoveled snow from our driveway
and knocked it off our shrubs and trees—sixty-two in all, for
I later counted them—until I began to feel weak and ex-
hausted. Four days later, while teaching a graduate seminar
at the seminary, I felt a tightening in the middle of my chest,
a tingling down my arms, and nausea and weakness. In the
hospital two hours later my doctor informed me that I had
a severe heart attack. I was confined to the hospital for a
month.

Ten years later I am enjoying good health, a wiser and,
I hope, a better man. I have attempted to profit from that
experience and take better care of my health. Also, I am
learning to accept my state of health with less anxiety, to
settle for more limited achievement, and to trust myself to
God's providential care.

A Theology of Health

The root meaning of health is wholeness. It means a fully-
functioning person, comparatively free of pain and anxiety.
It is doubtful whether anyone is a perfect specimen of health.
Most of us have some weakness, faults, failures, warped attitudes, prejudices, and perhaps some bodily handicap which
is always with us.

We are creatures living in the midst of a changing world,

an environment where there is cosmic evil and continual struggle for survival. T.S. Eliot wrote, "The world turns, and the world changes, but one thing never changes—the eternal struggle between good and evil."

The Bible has much to say about health and healing. The ancient Hebrews were concerned with the health of the whole man. They saw man as a unitary being, outer and inner man. The priestly documents of the Old Testament set forth numerous rules of health which have to do with both body and soul.

We conclude from God's dealings with human beings that he wants them to be healthy and happy. Jesus himself was called the Great Physician. We are told that he went about healing all manner of sickness and disease—the lame, the blind, and the diseased (Matt. 4:23; 9:35). He healed men and women and children. He was also concerned about mental health and emotional disturbances. He urged his followers not to be overly anxious about physical and material aspects of life, but to trust God for his providences.

I like the way the apostle John began his letter to his friend and colleague Gaius: "Beloved, I pray that all may go well with you and that you may be in health: I know that it is well with your soul" (3 John 2). What better thing could you wish for a friend than that he be in good health. Health is desired by everyone—health of body, mind, emotions, attitude, spirit.

Richard Dayrringer, chaplain, Baptist Hospital, Kansas City, Missouri, warns against faulty theological implications concerning illness. Struggling to understand God's involvement, or lack of it, in their illnesses, many people make inferences which are contrary to biblical teachings: "God does not know about me or care about me. God has sent this to punish and discipline me. God has let me down, for I do not deserve this. God is mad at me and is punishing me. My faith is gone, or else I would not feel alienated from God. If God will heal me, I will serve him." Obviously, these attitudes are based upon faulty concepts about the kind of God we serve. God is a loving Father. He is no respecter of persons, and his grace is offered to all who will accept it. God does know and care about our sickness.

Man is often responsible for his own illness. If he works too hard, eats too much, sleeps and rests too little, worries, drinks, and smokes, he must surely acknowledge that his sickness is at least partly due to his own neglect and sinning against his own body.

Although God does not send sickness upon us, he does permit us to be subject to disease. As free and responsible persons, we are subject to the problems of our world. We are not exempt because we are Christians. In his high-priestly prayer, Jesus did not pray that his disciples be taken out of the world, but that they should be strengthened against the powers of the evil one.

Sickness can be a learning experience. As a person faces life's crises, he can gain knowledge about himself, both his limitations and his strengths. If he is open to God's offer of grace, he can experience more of God's love and healing power. When a person learns what his limitations are and how to cope with them, he or she has gained one of life's greatest lessons.

Since God is concerned about my health, I must cooperate with him and his laws in the healing process. One's faith can play a large part in his recovery. By trusting God, we can appropriate all the resources he has provided for us. God's characteristic way of healing is not always immediate and obvious. He works through natural laws as applied by doctors, nurses, and others in the healing process. Even the breath of life is his miraculous gift. The patient who maintains hope, even in the face of frightening diagnosis or discouraging prognosis, has a better chance for recovery.

Chronic sickness or handicap may be your lot. Some people are born with a handicap which can never be removed. Through no fault of their own, or of anyone else, they are born to a life of physical limitation and pain. God did not cause this but simply permitted it in the midst of natural processes in a world of freedom where error and evil are active.

Paul had a "thorn in the flesh" which pained him severely. He prayed three times that God might remove it. God did not remove the thorn but said, "My grace is sufficient for you, for my power is made perfect in weakness" (2 Cor. 12:9). Paul had made up his mind to take pride in his weaknesses because they meant a deeper experience of the power of Christ. His very weakness made him strong in Christ.

I have a friend, past fifty years of age, who was born a cerebral palsy victim. No, not victim, but sufferer. In spite of severe limitations, she would never give in to her handicap. Her courage and faith have made her stronger than most Christians. Her example and witness provide inspiration and challenge to her many friends and acquaintances. She is a victorious Christian who never seems to feel sorry for herself.

Each person has the choice of standing up to evil and suffering rather than becoming its victim. George Buttrick has reminded us that the great "breakthrough" concerning the age-old problem of evil is the cross itself. Christ suffered and died on the cross, but he also rose again. His resurrection is our hope. Paul said, "If we suffer with Christ, we shall also reign with him" (2 Tim. 2:12).

Sickness As a Crisis

Sickness is a crisis experience. Something new is happening.

A turning point, a decisive moment is at hand. The Greek word for crisis means literally to separate, to pull apart. Medically, a crisis means a change pointing toward either recovery or death. There is urgency in every crisis; many times there is ultimate concern. The crisis may be a growth or learning experience, or it can be a deteriorating episode. It can lead to progress or to regression.

Physicians and psychiatrists tell us there is a predictable experience pattern as the individual faces a crisis. The normal growth pattern calls for struggle. This zigzag pattern of life includes smooth plateaus, rough dips, and upward thrusts. Many little dips are faced by the average person.

A crisis might be called a big dip, or a valley experience, one in which the individual has to call for outside help as he works through his problem. Such a crisis has both medical and theological implications. From the viewpoint of the Christian, it has been called the "dark night of the soul." Medically, it may be thought of as deep depression in which the patient ceases to be a fully-functioning person.

At the beginning of this chapter I mentioned my bout with a heart attack, which I consider was a major crisis. Later, as I analyzed my experience, I discovered it followed the pattern which psychiatrists and others in the medical profession say is usually observable in a major crisis.

I experienced the following steps in that crisis: (1) *Shock and denial.* At first, numbness; then: "I can't believe it; it must be a dream; it really isn't true." (2) *Irresponsibility and dependence.* Under sedation and oxygen I became wholly dependent upon others. A special nurse took over my existence. (3) *Anger.* Why me? Resentment at being dependent on others (orderlies, practical nurses, technicians) for feeding, baths, bedpans, enemas, medication. (4) *Analyzing the reasons for the attack.* Was I responsible? Too much physical exertion, being twenty pounds overweight, neglecting to keep my body strong, attempting too much work (driving long distances and preaching every weekend, in addition to teaching), worrying too much about family responsibilities. (5) *Mild depression:* guilt feelings over my carelessness, self-pity, and doubts. (6) *Acceptance of reality and call for help:* confession to God and others for my neglect, and acceptance of God's forgiveness. (7) *Responsibility and resolution:* making plans for recovery, exercising trust and hope, listening and praying to God. (8) *Celebration:* gratitude to God for recovery and for the help of other persons; and commitment to Christian vocation, with a new sense of my humanity and of God's grace.

Thanks be to God, if we are willing to learn from life's crises and trust ourselves to him and to our fellow human beings, his healing grace is available, and we can be shaped more and more into the likeness of Jesus Christ our Lord.

"Old" Is Not "Sick"

Being old and being sick are not the same thing. Many elderly people are vigorous and in good health. They are fully-functioning and enjoy life in the fullest sense. Of course, old age has its discomforts and sicknesses. Arthritic and digestive disturbances, dimming eyesight, diminished hearing, and other organic functions of the body undergo change.

Advancement in age also has its compensations healthwise—physically, mentally, and spiritually. The elderly do not seem to catch as many colds, are not subject to childhood diseases, often have gained a degree of immunity from other infectious diseases. Most of them have a rich store of knowledge and wisdom on how to stay reasonably healthy. And many have the spiritual capacity to live with sickness and to cope with the problems of suffering.

Today more people than ever before are living to advanced

age. Life is extended because many diseases—diphtheria, smallpox, polio, typhoid fever, cholera, to name a few—have virtually been wiped out. A person born today has a fifty-fifty chance of reaching the age of seventy-one. A woman who reaches sixty-five can look forward to attaining eighty-two, and a man at sixty-five has a chance of reaching seventy-eight. Rejoice! There is a lot of living and good health in the latter years.

The goal of aging is to have more wholeness of life, to become more mature in learning to live victoriously, even in the face of sicknesses. Being old can mean being a mature person who has known suffering and has learned to offer even that to God, whose power can transform it into something good and glorious.

The Choice Is Not Always Yours

We cannot always choose our state of health. In spite of all our precautions, sickness may still come to us. However, we can choose how we will react to our maladies.

Illnesses come in all forms and degrees: physical, intellectual, and emotional. Some are disabling. Many of them are chronic and not necessarily fatal. The important thing is to learn to live with what you have.

Physicians tell us the most common eye disease is the cataract. Surgery on cataracts is successful in about 90 to 95 percent of the time if the eyes are otherwise healthy. Doctors urge that this problem be cared for as soon as possible.

Among older people hearing often becomes impaired, although it may not be acute. Proper care of the ears by a physician will often keep down serious hearing problems. People should be encouraged to acquire hearing aids as needed.

Heart and lung disorders of many varieties are common among older people. Symptoms include shortness of breath, swelling of the legs and ankles, various types of chest pain, tightness across the chest, nausea, and sweating. With proper care, people may live many years with heart problems.

Numerous persons have troubles with digestion, especially as they grow older. Common problems include simple indigestion, peptic ulcer, severe pain in the stomach, bloating of the abdomen, gallbladder pains, constipation, hemorrhoids and other rectal problems, and diverticulitis in the lower abdomen.

Urinary diseases include problems with the kidneys, bladder, and prostate gland. Deteriorating kidney functions may produce uremia, a poisoning of the blood which can lead to death unless speedily corrected. Many elderly men have prostate gland trouble. The symptoms should be treated promptly before an emergency arises. If surgery is required, it need not cause undue anxiety, since it is usually a fairly simple operation.

The stroke is a common experience among older people. It is caused by an obstruction of the flow of blood to the brain. Symptoms vary from a simple temporary lapse of memory and temporary black-outs to complete paralysis of all the limbs. It may happen to one side of the body only. Speech may be affected, and one or more limbs may become weak. Many persons recover completely from a stroke. Others may be handicapped permanently. In any case, the individual should be encouraged to develop an attitude of courage and adventure in learning how to live with his condition.

The return of Cliff Arquette ("Charlie Weaver") to television after a lengthy battle to overcome a heart attack and a severe stroke, which rendered his left side almost useless, served as an inspiring example for us all, especially those who have experienced similar health hazards. His courage and persistent effort showed how one man extended his usefulness in society in the face of great difficulty. In addition to perform-

ing as a humorist, Arquette was also recognized for his creative
works in oil painting. In reality, he was truly as alive in spirit
as the mischievous "Charlie Weaver" he portrayed.

Some people are born with physical handicaps; others are
afflicted with them later on in life. In either case, one must
learn to live with his limitation. During his college days a
friend of mine climbed into a tree to thresh pecans. Losing
his grip, he fell and broke his back. From that point on, he
wore braces, walked with crutches, and used a wheelchair.
He accepted the handicap as a challenge. His life became
an inspiration to all who knew him. He finished college, took
a doctor's degree from the seminary, served as a teacher in
a college, and became a denominational leader, especially in
the area of the rural church. He is now about seventy years
of age. He climaxed his career as a professor in a seminary
where he influenced the lives of hundreds of young ministers.

Mind and body are closely related in times of health and
sickness. One's mental attitude can have great effect upon
the healing process. Doctors agree that many illnesses are
psychosomatic, that body symptoms are often related to mental
and emotional stress. Certain disorders, such as stomach ulcers,
ulcerated colitis, some heart palpitations or heart pains, arthritis, high blood pressure, certain severe headaches, and other
physical symptoms may be due in part, at least, to emotional
tension.

We should not try to diagnose ourselves in times of illness.
Only medically trained persons can determine these problems.
Everyone should seek professional help from family physician,
and other specialists as advisable, including psychologists and
psychiatrists.

One can determine to keep a healthy attitude of mind. The
older person especially has many assets which can help him
remain healthy and also cope with sickness when it comes.

He has the advantage of judgment acquired by experience. Also, he may have gained freedom over the self-conscious anxieties of youth. Poise and self-control have been achieved because he has found inner peace. A healthy state of mind can help the body cooperate in the healing process. It is a fact that one can often act himself into a way of thinking as well as think himself into a way of acting.

Coping with Senility

Not all elderly people are senile. The symptoms of senility are often confused with those of arteriosclerosis, or hardening of the arteries. Medical science has discovered this process begins in youth and progresses normally to old age. Restriction of the arteries slows down blood circulation to the brain which in turn can retard the mental processes. Fatty deposits in certain arteries may predispose people to strokes, heart attacks, and other serious illnesses. Dieting and medication are frequently used to relieve arteriosclerosis.

The term "senility" is often applied to mental and emotional difficulties. It is not the same thing as arteriosclerosis, but we are told the two may be related. Senility may be accelerated when a person ceases the active use of mental faculties. If he withdraws and gives up, the mind will degenerate more rapidly.

Symptoms of senility range from mild problems with memory to severe violent reactions: loss of recent memory, repetitiousness, slow thinking, distortion of facts, impaired judgment, rigidity of opinions, persecution complex, irrational conversation, wearing of soiled clothing, loss of orientation as to time, person, place, or all three, hostility, loss of control of personal habits, and violent displays of anger.

How can we deal with apparent increasing senility in elderly family members? The facts of physical change cannot be denied, but certain guidelines may be helpful in coping with these changes. Medication will sometimes promote better circulation by reducing corrosion in the blood vessels, thus improving mental functions of the individual. Sound medical help should be sought in dealing with these problems.

We should accept the older person for what he is and not resent the changes observable in him. Accept his bodily functions for what they are, and do not put value judgments on them.

Avoid making impossible demands of the senile person as if he were still fully-functioning and self-sufficient. Do not expect him to remember as he once did. However, help him keep in touch with reality by refusing to encourage or participate in his fantasies or delusions. Keep things routine as far as possible, thus avoiding the necessity for the older person to change constantly. Regularity in schedules may avoid much confusion.

Freedom of mobility should be provided the older person. Brief walks or automobile rides may help him maintain contact with reality. Include him in social contacts and conversations.

The aging person himself may also find ways of coping with senility. One may develop strong psychological defenses against the malady. Dr. James Folsom of the Veterans' Administration, Washington, D.C., and other experts have suggested certain techniques which may be helpful. Be active. Do. not spend all your time in a comfortable chair. Eat properly. Take time to obtain the right foods. Keep up your interests. One woman, eighty-two, gets up at 5:30 A.M. and reads current literature for two or three hours to keep her mind alert. Control stress as far as possible. Relax. Get adequate sleep. Stretch out and really sleep deeply. Consciously resolve to pick up new concepts, and try to live in the present. Do things for other persons. Look outward. Refuse to spend time in self-pity. Do not fret about loss of memory. Minor memory losses really begin at about age forty. Practice reality-orientation. This is a group process in which the individual can reawaken usable parts of the brain and develop new ways of functioning.[1]

Doctor and Patient

Through the centuries the family physician has been indispensable for healthful living. A medical doctor is trained to understand physical and emotional symptoms. His ministry includes diagnosis (determining the nature and extent of the illness), prescribing treatment for the illness, and prognosis (predicting the probable future course of a disorder).

Preventive health is his ideal. Every person should have regular check-ups and certainly see his physician as soon as he discovers some symptom of illness. Self-treatment is usually not advisable, for it can be fatal.

Physicians are human beings also and have their personal problems and limitations. They need understanding and support and comfort. In choosing a doctor, the patient and family should consider the following: Is he capable? Is he available? Is he affable?

The family physician can treat disease himself or offer counsel when a specialist is needed. In this day of specialization doctors work together in providing the specific kind of treatment needed. A doctor may call in a urologist (kidney specialist), a gynecologist (specialist in female organs and diseases), cardiologist (a heart specialist), gastroenterologist (stomach specialist), orthopedist (joint and bone specialist), opthalmologist (eye specialist), ear, nose and throat specialist, geriatrician (specialist in diseases of old age), and others as needed.

Do you know how to relate to a doctor? Are you considerate of him? One doctor offers the following practical suggestions for relating to one's physician: Do not call a doctor at home except in an emergency. He is usually tired and needs rest. Accept a substitute in an emergency if your doctor is not available. Discuss your physician's availability with him. Learn what you can expect from him. See your physician regularly, as often as necessary to keep him familiar with your needs. Be considerate of your doctor as a human being. He likes small courtesies also. Accept your doctor's diagnosis without requiring full details. Leave this to his judgment.

Do not change doctors simply because of a misunderstanding. Stay with your doctor unless there are serious reasons for changing. Do not dismiss a physician simply because he made a mistake. Perhaps the only good reasons for asking a physician to withdraw are: if he repeatedly fails to do what he promises he will do; if he does not show proper concern for the patient; or if he plainly lacks the dignity, propriety, and ordinary competence of a doctor.

Make appointments before going to the doctor. Keep appointments on time, and try to be reasonably patient if you have to wait. Furnish the doctor with all the necessary information about the patient as to diet, medicines, and so forth.

The Art of Acceptance

If one is sick, that is a fact. He cannot ignore it or pretend that he does not hurt. The earlier he is willing to accept the fact of illness, the sooner he can learn to cope with it. A part of the struggle to get well is in dealing with the reality.

We must be willing to accept help from others. There is a subtle temptation for us to allow our resentment toward ourselves or the situation to spill over in our attitude toward those who offer to help us. Accepting help is as legitimate as giving help. The difference is that we are now on the receiving side of human sharing. Let us thank God for it and show appreciation toward those who minister to us.

We can learn from sickness. Pain can have a cleansing effect on life. Suffering can be accepted as a vocation, as a calling to measure up to what life demands. Pain also can give insight. It has much to teach.

It is possible to use affliction rather than being used up by affliction. The psalmist testified, "It is good for me that I have been afflicted, that I might learn thy statutes" (Psalm 119:71). Paul wrote, "Our light affliction works for us a more exceeding weight of eternal glory" (2 Cor. 4:17). In some mysterious way God takes the suffering offered up to him and transforms it into something glorious.

Regardless of our situation or state of health, we should try to offer each day to God in worship: "This is the day which the Lord has made; let us rejoice and be glad in it" (Psalm 118:24). "We are more than conquerors through Christ who loves us and gives himself for us" (Rom. 8:28-29).

This message from an unknown writer spoke to me many years ago:

> I walked a mile with Pleasure,
>   She chattered all the way,
> But left me none the wiser
>   For all she had to say.

> I walked a mile with Sorrow,
>   And ne'er a word said she;
> But, oh, the things I learned from her
>   When Sorrow walked with me!

7 *Death, Be Not Proud*

John Donne, English preacher-poet of the seventeenth century, wrote:

> Death, be not proud, though some have called
>   thee
> Mighty and dreadful, for thou art not so:
> For those whom thou think'st thou dost overthrow
> Die not, poor Death; nor yet canst thou kill me.
>
> . . . .
>
> One short sleep past, we wake eternally,
> And death shall be no more; death, thou shalt die!

Have you ever faced up to your own death? One day it will come, and there is no way of avoiding it. One writer reminds us that we may deny death or postpone it, but its coming is inevitable. Sooner or later we all must experience death. If we are prepared for it, we can face it victoriously and courageously, and even joyfully.

I had not really faced up to my own death until I had that heart attack in January, 1964. At fifty-six I experienced my first encounter with death. In a hospital bed, under an oxygen tent, I honestly looked death in the face and came away the victor. I did not really think I would die at that time, but I had to be honest—it was a possibility.

How did I cope with the experience? I was not afraid to die, but I did not *want* to die. I felt I had "miles to go and promises to keep" before I called it a day. Fannie Mae and I had enjoyed life so much together. Surely we must have some more wonderful years left with and for each other. I wanted to see our two sons and one daughter well established in their vocations. I dreamed of happy times with grandchildren. I wanted further to serve in teaching and writing and pastoring.

But death was a possibility. Here was a concrete reality—only a short distance between life and death. Only a few heartbeats could make the difference. Looking death in the face, I found myself singing Psalm 27, which I had learned years before as a voice student. Quietly I sang, for I did not want to disturb anyone else in the hospital, "The Lord is my light and my salvation; whom shall I fear? The Lord is the strength of my life; of whom shall I be afraid?"

God did bless and give strength. Six months later I was able to go to Beirut, Lebanon, on a sabbatical leave which had been planned for a long time. That year of teaching in our Arab Baptist Seminary and extensive travel in the Middle East was sheer therapeutic joy. Now, ten years later, I thank God every morning for the gift of life one more day.

Are You Afraid to Die?

In a sense, it is normal for human beings to fear death. Since life is a gift, it is natural for man to hold on to that gift and to resist its being taken from him. There is a sense in which the Bible considers death an enemy—an enemy because it seeks to take away the gift of life which comes from God.

Death involves fear of the unknown. We have never experienced death, and so it is strange and mysterious. This step has never been taken before. There is fear of the loss of one's body. The biological is the most obvious aspect of personhood. Sickness and pain, and especially death, are a threat to the body. These things may disfigure and impair, and even take away its normal functions. The love of self includes the love of one's body. As disease progresses, one fears the loss of control of the mental faculties as well as the physical organs. This loss of control creates a threat to personal integrity, and, therefore, may produce deep fear.

During a period of serious illness, there is always the fear of loneliness, a sense of isolation for oneself. Many people tend to avoid seriously ill persons. This withdrawal is even more pronounced during the process of dying. The presence of death reminds us how close our own death may be. The individual is deprived of the support and contact to which he has been accustomed, the human nurture which he needs from others.

Also one may fear the loss of family and friends. The dying person, as well as his family, needs to work through the grief experience so that acknowledging the separation can be accomplished even before death.[1]

The fear of the loss of self-identity is perhaps the greatest fear of all. The loss of human contact, of family and friends, of body structure and function, of self-control and total consciousness—all threaten the sense of who I am. Man has an innate sense of the continuity of life, the on-goingness of human relationships, and the eternal dimension of existence. Therefore, it is a natural reaction to want to hold on to life, and thus fear the loss of it.

Life and Death Are One

The Lebanese philosopher-poet-mystic Khalil Gibran wrote, "Life and death are one, even as the river and the sea are one."

The answer to fear is hope. And this hope is provided by a Christian faith that enables one to accept death without being dominated by fear. Death of the physical body is not final. We look forward to the resurrection when we shall be alive forevermore.

In Eugene O'Neill's drama entitled *Long Day's Journey into Night* every member of the family experienced only darkness in the tragic events that unfolded. They were encountering death in the midst of life. In their view, the future offered no hope. There was only darkness ahead, a difficult journey ending in night.

On the other hand, from a Christian perspective, a better title for life's pilgrimage would be "Long Night's Journey into Day." For the person of faith, there is light ahead. As well as experiencing death in the midst of life, he also is experiencing life in the midst of death. We must learn to relate death and life, to know the meaning of death in the midst of life and the meaning of life in the face of death. A person starts dying the day he is born. But he also starts living and experiencing life in the face of death. Life was created to win out ultimately.

Accepting the normal aging process will help one face up to death realistically. He can make peace with death because life reaches beyond, through the reality of the resurrection.

A Christian view of death deals with the meaning of life and the continuation of life after death. It also has something to say about the death event. First, it is a natural event. It has been called a monstrous reality which cannot be dodged. Man was created finite and mortal. Therefore, death is the natural end of finite life.[2]

In the second place, death is a personal event. It is a unique reality in the life of each individual. There is a sense in which it must be encountered alone. Faced with the end of life, one is forced to examine the totality of his life. My death is not simply a vital statistic. For me it is personal and meaningful. And I must accept it step by step until it has run its course.

Death is also a social event. I am an individual in the midst of a community. I am a part of family, the church, and the wider human fellowship. Death breaks into these relationships and, therefore, affects the whole community.

Finally, we have to admit that death is a mystery. We know little about it personally. It is related to creation and to the whole universe of living creatures and things. It is a part of God's total creative enterprise. Only by faith in the purpose of God can we experience something of the hope of life after death.

One's attitude toward life and death makes a difference in the way he copes with death. A proper sense of death ought to make life more meaningful. John Killinger reminds us that life is of God, and it is meant to be lived fully and freely. Death does not destroy him who has lived or what he has stood for; it only brings to a close this segment of his existence.

Learning How to Die

Mrs. Norma McDermott always made me feel good when I went to visit her in the nursing home. In her middle seventies, she had suffered severe strokes which limited her ability to communicate. She was always grateful for visits and complained very little. One day she and I were sharing some of the joys and activities of the younger members of our families. Norma looked straight into my eyes and said, "They are learning how to live, and I am learning how to die." "And we have to learn how to do both, don't we?" I asked. She replied, "Yes, we do." I have pondered that profound insight many times. We do have to learn how to die.

Robert Neal, professor of psychiatry and religion at Union

Theological Seminary, New York, understands death as being a natural part of life.[3] In his relationship with people who are either dying or have come close to death, Neal discovered that for these people food takes on a new taste, music, a new dimension, life, a greater fullness. Learning how to die will give us a sense of trust, and we will find life more joyful and peaceful and less frightening.

Recently, our church had a six-week seminar for adults on death and grief. In a general assembly we first discussed some aspect of the subject, and then we broke up into small groups and faced up to our own death by participating in the following exercises. (1) Write a description of a grief experience you have had in the loss of a loved one. (2) Express on paper your feelings about facing your own death. Are you ready? Do you fear it? (3) Write out your own obituary, giving the facts, some goals you have reached, and some things you have left unfinished. (4) Outline a funeral service you feel would be helpful for your own family and others. (5) Compose a statement of your Christian faith about death and hope.

During this entire seminar the attendance was large. Participants ranged in age from twenty to eighty years. The interest was high, and the personal sharing heart-warming. We all felt we were better able to face up to our own deaths and the grief process experienced in the death of loved ones.

Life is a pilgrimage, not a meaningless circle. Death is a part of that pilgrimage. We experience both life and death continually throughout our pilgrimage. Life begins as a small cell which grows and divides; old cells die; new cells are born. Life, death, and resurrection happen as a life process. The death of the body is a part of that process.

Rather than denying death, let us see it as a reality which must be faced. Dr. Elizabeth Kubler-Ross's book *On Death and Dying* helped me to learn more about the art of dying.[4]

She found that as people approach death they go through the following stages: *denial*—"It can't happen to me"; *anger*— "Why me?"; *bargaining*—"Yes, me, but"; *depression*—"I need help"; *acceptance*—death is a reality, and I accept my own death as inevitable. Dr. Kubler-Ross believes we should live life today and enjoy it, and also learn to face up to our own finitude in the younger years of life. We ought not wait until we are on our deathbed to learn these lessons.

Dying with Dignity

In his own home one day Mr. Jim Smith, seventy-six years of age and in failing health, said to me, "I am not afraid to die, but I do fear the manner in which I may die." He went on to say that he did not want to be helpless and dependent on others for a long period of time. "I don't want my wife to have to wear herself out waiting on me. I'd rather go quickly when the time comes." I agreed that this would be the ideal thing if we had a choice.

As a matter of fact, however, we cannot choose the time or the manner of our own death. It may come suddenly with a massive heart attack, or it may come gradually in the form of a long bout with cancer or a series of small strokes. Recently, two women died on the same day, one of a sudden heart attack at the age of eighty-five, and another of a brain tumor which had taken her gradually and slowly over a period of two years of confinement. Neither these persons nor the families had any choice in the manner of their dying.

Dying with dignity means many things. It means no person should have to die alone—without the fellowship of significant persons who care. Regardless of his age and condition, one has the right to the best medical care possible. He deserves to be treated as a person all the way to the end of his pilgrimage. When people are no longer able to communicate verbally, often they are still able to understand the warmth and care which others offer. They deserve love and respect even in this limited condition.

Many feeble old people lose muscular and nerve control over their bladder or bowels. This is called incontinence and is often associated with disease of bladder, prostate, or bowel. This condition is usually more pronounced in bedridden patients.

The incontinent and helpless patient deserves good nursing care and should be treated with dignity and compassion. They should be kept dry and comfortable by frequent changing of clothing and bed linens and careful bathing and powdering. Ordinarily parents are not impatient with infants who are helpless and dependent upon them. All who minister to incontinent adults should strive for the same patience and compassion which is practiced in the care of infants.

A person has a right to know what his physical condition is—his medical diagnosis and its probable prognosis. In the face of terminal illness, most patients want to know their condition. In fact, most of them usually know their diagnosis whether they are formally told or not.[5] Families and patients often play games with one another by withholding facts. Both are usually relieved when they are open and honest enough to face the realities.

When a patient asks for the facts, usually he should be told the truth. Doctors and family members should work together in honest communication with the terminal patient. Occasionally, a patient will not want to be told the truth. One businessman, about eighty years of age, informed his family that if he ever had a terminal illness, he did not want to be told about it. They honored his wishes and did not discuss it, even though he suffered several months with cancer. When I visited him, I felt the visits could have been more meaningful if we both had been open and honest with each other. However, as a human being he had the right to his own choice. We shared our Christian faith and hope but never discussed the possibility of his death.

Does a person have a right to refuse treatment when he is terminally ill? This question is being debated widely at present. For example, an eighty-year-old man may choose not to have surgery, even though he knows he will die without it. The choice should be made jointly by doctor and patient and family.

The extension of life by artificial means is a modern achievement of medical science. It is often accomplished, however, with extreme financial burden to the family and/or the welfare department. Some patients may prefer death by natural means rather than the extension of life by artificial procedures. It may come down to the question of the quality of life rather than the length of it. For example, when brain damage has been so great as to render the person incapable of mental processes, it may be better to permit him to die naturally than to go on breathing artificially when he is no longer capable of living a conscious existence.

Every person has a right to decide these matters before he comes to that terminal stage. The elderly person who cannot eat may prefer to die a natural death rather than being kept alive by forced feeding. Temporary use of oxygen is a tool of medical science. However, continuous use of oxygen with the hopelessly ill may only prolong the agony of dying. One doctor says in the battle with death there is the desire to "do something." The physician must decide whether fluids, oxygen, and various tubes are desirable. Quite often the wiser course is to do relatively little, according to this doctor.

I have talked with my own family about dying with dignity and have requested that I be permitted to die a natural death without the use of artificial means of prolonging life, in the event I should come to that helpless condition in which I am no longer a conscious, living human being. In the case of terminal illness, when reasonable hope for recovery is gone, I do not want a helpless body to be forced into living and suffering and causing further suffering for my family. We have already talked this over so that it will not have to be faced for the first time should such a crisis arise.

The closing phases of life often are not associated with much suffering. During all phases of impending death the physician, family, patient, and others should work together to minimize physical discomfort and feelings of loneliness, anxiety, and fear. According to one doctor, the excessive use of drugs, mechanical devices, and other measures may mean "procrastination with regard to death rather than prolongation of life." [6]

The Christian Funeral

Dr. George W. Truett was pastor of First Baptist Church in Dallas, Texas, for over forty years. As a young pastor in the suburban town of Garland, Texas, I grew to admire and love him dearly. In the last months of his life, he suffered from a malignancy which gradually took his strength away. When he died, I grieved with multitudes of other persons.

The funeral service was a mixture of sorrow and joy, but the predominant note was joy because of the Christian hope his life exemplified. A men's quartet sang two hymns, "Rock of Ages" and "O Love That Will Not Let Me Go." Suffering and love had been the two dominant themes of his life. Thousands of people assembled to pay tribute to a great man and to mourn with his family and his church. In a sense, it was a glorious experience. God was there in presence, and we had the assurance that George W. Truett was victorious in the face of death.

The primary purpose of a funeral service is to focus on the meaning of life and to encourage persons in grief to accept God's claim upon their lives and seek comfort in his grace. It is a ritual act in which the church shows its concern for those who suffer loss. The congregation offers fellowship in an effort to strengthen the grief-stricken in the crisis of death. The funeral also can be an appropriate memorial for the person who has died.

Edgar Jackson, who has made special studies in the area of grief work, summarizes the requirements of a Christian funeral. He says it should recognize and meet the needs of the participants, be aware of the powerful emotions at work, face reality rather than deny it, acknowledge the validity of grief work, provide opportunity for religious community to give its spiritual support, and encourage the great affirmations of Christian faith.[7]

Affirming Life After Death

At ninety-three years of age, Miss Beulah Emory encountered a serious illness. For days she hovered between life and death. Finally, she survived and became fairly active again, for one her age. She said that she actually walked through the valley of the shadow of death and right on up to the gates of heaven. When she got there, the keepers of the portals said, "We are not ready for you yet. You will have to return." She declared that when she was fully conscious again, the 23rd Psalm appeared on the wall of her hospital room, and she read it all the way through. She reported, "when I walked through the valley of the shadow, I really was not alone; God was with me." Then she added, "I wish God had let me go on home, but I am willing to stay here and do whatever he has for me to do." Miss Beulah is certain there is life after death for the Christian, for she has had a foretaste of it.

The good news of the gospel tells us that Christ came into the world to teach men how to live and how to die. The purpose of his coming was "that they may have life and have it abundantly." There is no conflict between living abundantly and dying appropriately.

The great affirmation of life is found in the resurrection of Jesus, God's affirmation of life over death. Eugene O'Neill wrote a play entitled *Lazarus Laughed*. He saw Lazarus coming out of the grave laughing, a sort of joyous laugh which affirmed life. Lazarus testified there is only one life. There is only one laughter—the laughter of God. There is no death really. Death is a portal, a passageway into deeper and brighter life. There is only life. Therefore, we must learn to live, celebrate, love, accept, affirm.

Khalil Gibran asked, "What is it to cease breathing but to free the breath from its restless tides that it may rise and expand and seek God unencumbered? And when you have reached the mountaintop, then you shall begin to climb. And when the earth shall claim your limbs, then shall you truly dance."

Charles A. Lindbergh, world-famous aviator, known as the "Lone Eagle" because of his non-stop flight to Paris as a young man, died August 26, 1974, past eighty years of age. He wrote the following words for use at his funeral: "We commit the body of General Charles A. Lindbergh to its final resting place, but his spirit we commend to Almighty God, knowing that death is but a new adventure in existence and remembering how Jesus said upon the cross, 'Father, into thy hands I commend my spirit.' "

Is it any wonder Paul mocked death: "O death, where is thy victory? O death, where is thy sting? . . . Thanks be unto God, who gives us the victory through our Lord Jesus Christ" (1 Cor. 15:55-57).

8 *The Best Is Yet to Be*

Recently I read a book entitled *My First One Hundred Years*.[1] Dr. Emmet Reid, professor emeritus and research chemist, Johns Hopkins University, wrote the book during his ninety-ninth year. In the prologue he declared, "I've seen a lot of things, and I haven't quit looking, but it's time to make an interim report." His grandfather was a Baptist pastor in the mountains of Georgia, and in 1857 his father went as a Baptist missionary to what is now Nigeria. Reid's Christian heritage is evident in his own life.

In the epilogue, this centenarian provides an example of vibrant living for all of us: "On the whole, life has been pleasant. Work is the greatest blessing God ever gave to man, and I am fortunate that I always had interesting work to do. The way to keep active is to keep active." Obviously, Emmet Reid still finds life exciting after one hundred years of it.

Browning really was right. He could believe "the best is yet to be" because he saw "the last of life, for which the first was made." Because of his trust in God, he could see all, look life full in the face, and not be afraid.

I keep resolving, year by year, to live life in the present, to celebrate life by giving thanks to God for each day. The psalmist said, "Bless the Lord, o my soul, and all that is within me, bless his holy name" (Psalm 103:1). We can celebrate in memory all past blessings, celebrate in awareness of present blessings, and celebrate in anticipation of our blessed future hope. Let us resolve to make the quality of the temporary worthy of the eternal. God's gift of eternal life comes one day at a time. Let us savor this morsel of eternity now.

How do you see your life now, its beginning, its middle, its ending? Someone has suggested that if our roots are struck deep, present living may make a mockery of the beginning and the ending of life. It is life itself that counts, not how it begins or ends. Let something new be born in your life—a new thing to see, a new action to be taken, a new person to love. It is not how long we live, but how much, how well, how deeply!

The person who has found purpose in life by anchoring his faith in God will continue to discover meaning in all of life's experiences. Someone has said, "Tell me your view of the universe, and I will tell you the meaning of your life." In his poem "The Death of the Hired Man" Robert Frost spoke of the purposelessness of the hired man's life. He had "nothing to look backward to with pride, nothing to look forward to with hope." One who has lived with purpose looks backward with satisfaction and forward with hope. There are more blessings ahead.

Perhaps the greatest difference between the earlier years and the retirement years is the difference in perspective. The earlier years focus upon work and production, the reaching of outer objectives and goals. The retirement years center on the enrichment of the inner life, the attainment of new, spiritual goals. Life must be evaluated by different criteria insofar as vocation, stewardship of time and money, active participation, and physical activity are concerned.

If life had meaning for God in its beginning and in the middle years, it has meaning at the end. In *Learn to Grow*

Old Paul Tournier says the older person needs a "redirection of ambition." Human power is now inner-directed rather than outer-directed.

Coming to Terms with Time

How one relates to time is one of life's greatest challenges. Among the problems of old age is a general fear of time. Time is one aspect of existence which is beyond man's control. In his younger years he does not reflect upon its meaning, and in old age it may become a scary nightmare.

Time is God's gift, meant for man's intelligent use. The Greek New Testament uses three different words for time. The word *chronos* has to do with the passing of time chronologically. The term *kairos* refers to a fixed time with purpose as seen in the "time of harvest," the time of opportunity. As Jesus came toward the end of his life and saw the cross as God's purpose for redemption, he said, "My time is at hand" (Matt. 26:18). Paul realized the evil forces at work in society and exhorted his fellow Christians to "redeem the time" (Eph. 5:16). The term *eschaton* refers to the end-time or the "last things" as we come to God's judgment day. Jesus said, "I am the *alpha* and *omega*, the beginning and the end" (Rev. 22:13).

I would like to learn to live in time and not run away from it. Every day has meaning. How wisely God has ordained that we live one day at a time! If one imagined all the problems that could face him in old age, he would be overwhelmed by the prospect. But if he deals with one problem at a time, one day at a time, as it arrives, life is manageable.

Time produces change. We should be on guard against the "foreshortened time" syndrome, the feeling that time has run out for us. We still have time to plan, to dream, to participate. Time and change are a challenge, not a menace or a defeat.

An old philosopher once said, "You can't step into the same

river twice." You see, the river moves on, and at your next step it will be different. It will have changed. Since time is ever changing, I must change with it. If I stubbornly resist it, I shall be disappointed and defeated. If I accept it and yield to its power, I can roll with the tide toward life's great objective. I do not belong primarily to the past but to the present. I want to be open to the present and to what it offers. Thus, I shall be ready for the future.

Learning to live with leisure is one way of coming to terms with time. No longer are there fixed hours and planned schedules. I am challenged to deal with time on my own. Leisure time can bring great compensations—relaxation versus tension, enjoyment versus drudgery, reaping rewards versus mere striving. Perhaps I need to get rid of my clock and calendar, and really accept time as it comes.

As one grows older he should have a more mature view of time. Indeed, he must learn to sanctify time, acknowledge it as God's gift, a moment in which a man meets God, when he is aware of the importance of eternity in his own life. Every moment ought to be lived in relationship to eternity, filled with quality rather than mere quantity. One must not permit the years to imprison life, but rather to free life so that each day may be lived as a joyous gift from God.

Since time is God's gift, then time means worship. To worship God is to find fulfillment in time and assurance for eternity. As one writer has indicated, it takes three things to attain a sense of significant being: God, a soul, and a moment. And the three are always here. Just to *be* is a blessing. Just to *live* is holy. I have found inspiration in these lines by Dag Hammarskjold:

> Lord, thine the day,
> And I the day's.

Pursuing Life's Interests

All through our lives many things bring delight to us. Words-
worth found delight in a rainbow:

> My heart leaps up when I behold
> A rainbow in the sky:
> So was it when my life began,
> So is it now I am a man,
> So be it when I shall grow old,
>   Or let me die!

In a sermon many years ago, Harry Emerson Fosdick reminded his congregation that some things never wear out. The
love of nature is one of those abiding gifts of life. I recall
my first taste of nature as a small child, sitting on a hillside
amid flowers waving in the summer breeze, watching a ruby-
throated hummingbird sipping nectar from the flowers. I still
get excited walking among the wild flowers near my home
and count it a treasure when I see a hummingbird flitting
about, especially a ruby-throated one.

The *love of reading* is another of life's treasures that never
wears out. Do you recall when you first developed that love?
The person is fortunate who has learned the friendship of good
books, for that never can be taken away from him. Perhaps
it is poetry—by Longfellow, Lowell, Browning, Tennyson,
Frost, Sandburg, T.S. Eliot, or Dylan Thomas. Charles Kingsley
once said, "Except a living man, there is nothing more wonderful than a book." Milton agreed: "A good book is the precious
lifeblood of a master spirit."

A ninety-year-old friend, confined to a nursing home, continued to enjoy reading. One day I found him poring over
a large-print copy of *Reader's Digest*. He also had a large-print
Bible from which he found daily inspiration. Having read the
Bible through many times, he declared he never got tired of

searching its pages.

Perhaps the *love of art* kindled in you during early childhood, abides as a rich deposit in your senior years. Art collections and museums still feed the spirit and are worth making the effort to visit them again and again.

I can never forget Thorwaldsen's *Christus* in a small church in Copenhagen. Located along the sides of the church are statues of the twelve apostles created by the great artist. Behind the altar stands the famous statue of Christ, looking down upon the worshiper, Only by kneeling and looking up can one see the expression of compassion on the Lord's face.

No one who has seen Michaelangelo's *Moses* in the Church of St. Peter in Chains, Rome, can forget its lesson in strength and wisdom. It is surpassed only by the artist's magnificent *David* in Florence. And you cannot doubt that Michaelangelo really experienced both "agony" and "ecstasy" as you behold the majesty of the ceiling in the Sistine Chapel of St. Peter's in Rome.

Since childhood I have been enthralled with Leonardo da Vinci's *Last Supper*. I had heard many stories and used illustrations about it in sermons. I did not realize how much a part of me it had become until I saw the original painting in Milan, Italy, in 1972. When I stepped inside the one-time refectory of the old church and stood in the presence of the masterpiece, to my surprise, I could not control my emotions. Tears filled my eyes. I felt overwhelmed. You see, the love and lessons of the *Last Supper* continue to bless my life as long as I live.

Recently, I visited an artist who is past three-score-years-and-ten. As I walked into her home studio, I felt I wanted to be silent for a moment. Beautiful paintings surrounded the room. I exclaimed, "How beautiful!" She said quietly, her eyes dancing, "This is my life! I am very happy with it. I am satisfied with life."

What are the things that never wear out in your experience? Take time out to conjure them up. Review their meaning. Encounter them again. Pursue them further. I would like to visit the Sistine Chapel again. I am sure I shall visit often our local Museum of Western Art and the Kimbell Art Museum of classical and contemporary masterpieces.

You may want to take up new interests, to do some things you have never had time to do before. As you might guess, I am trying my hand at oil painting for the first time in my life. I have no delusions of producing great art; I just want to do it for the joy it brings me. I am already convinced I will never be a "Grandpa Moses," but there is something about mixing colors and spreading on the canvas what one feels inside that brings great satisfaction.

The broader one's interests, the greater his enjoyment of the retirement years. Perhaps you will want to pursue your own special interest—reading, gardening, golfing, writing, listening to music, composing music, traveling, forming new friendships, sewing, continuing your education in a college class, or a thousand other things that provide reasons for living. Try something new!

Cultivating a Sense of Humor

The ability to laugh at ourselves can help us accept the trials as well as the joys of life. Some of the world's great comedians have capitalized on unattractive physical appearances or handicaps by turning them into assets. Jimmy Durante, with a wagging finger and a jaunty toss of the head, has created a million laughs by calling attention to his big "schnozz."

During the Lincoln-Douglas debates, Lincoln's sense of humor doubtless helped him finally win the presidency. When Douglas accused him of being two-faced, Lincoln pointed his long finger toward his own face and said, "It's the face my Maker gave me, and, for better or for worse, it's the only one I have. Do you think I'd go around holding it up in front of you if I had another one?" Lincoln was humble enough to laugh at himself.

During his White House years, President Harry Truman often told people: "The older I get, the better I seem to be able to laugh at my own foolishness and weaknesses." One day he met an older acquaintance, whose eyesight was failing. This friend greeted the President, "Oh, it's you, Senator." President Truman restrained himself for the time being, but when out of earshot of his friend, he let out a big laugh at his own expense.

Recently Alice Roosevelt Longworth, daughter of President Theodore Roosevelt, revealed she still has her sense of humor. Sometimes called Princess Malice because of her mischievous spirit, she refuses to live in the past. "Nostalgia? Goodness, no! What more interesting time than this?" Reading helps her keep alert and alive. Now she avows lightly, "the tooth of time is gnawing at this ancient carcass." Her father used to say, "I can either run the country or control Alice—but not both." Someone remarked, "Theodore Roosevelt took the easy way out. He ran the country." [2]

A sense of humor can help the aged person laugh at himself and make use of the ludicrous in life's amusing experiences. In a writers' conference, a retired woman shared an experience which delighted all of us. A friend of hers past eighty years of age asked, "Will you take me shopping? I haven't been for quite a while, and I am simply running out of fig leaves." Then there was the proud grandmother who joined humor with ambition. When asked the age of her grandsons, she replied, "Well, the doctor is two, and the lawyer is four."

Maturing in Christian Virtues

Dr. Ethel Percy Andrus, founder of National Retired Teachers' Association and American Association of Retired Persons, once said, "We do not grow old. We become old by not growing." A human being should continue to grow as long as he lives. When he comes to adulthood, he will cease to grow physically, to be sure, but he should keep on growing mentally and spiritually. I want my zest for living to continue right on to the end of my pilgrimage. And perhaps we shall take up on the other side of death where we leave off here on earth. I feel a responsibility to God, to myself, and to my fellowman to remain open to life and to the road ahead.

Sydney J. Harris, a popular columnist, said, "We older people like to prate a lot about the duties and responsibilities of young people, but we have an obligation upon us by growing older." We have the obligation to become more appealing on the inside although we may become less attractive on the outside. An older person who gets all dried up and brittle and wrinkled and full of complaints is a total drag. "Growing older imposes a duty upon us to get more like a peach on the inside as we get more like a prune on the outside," Harris added. We have to become mellower, more tolerant, more perceptive, and wiser to compensate for the external ravages of the aging process.

Young people have a love and appreciation for oldsters who have maintained a spirit of youth within themselves. An octogenarian who is both childlike and wise, spirited and supportive, more willing to learn than he is quick to advise, can be a delightful person. Harris also reminds us: "Socrates began taking dancing lessons at seventy; most of us just take dying lessons."

I like the spirit of the Old Testament character Caleb, one

of Joshua's colleagues sent by Moses to spy out the land of Canaan. Forty years later, at eighty-five years of age, he came to Joshua and asked for his portion of the new land. He requested "the mountain territory, the land of giants who live in great fortified cities." It is exciting to hear this elderly man declare: "I am as good as I was forty years ago! I am as strong to this day as I was in the day that Moses sent me to spy out the land. My strength now is as my strength was then, for war, for going and coming. So now give me this mountain territory. Give me one more mountain to conquer! It may be that the Lord will be with me, and I shall drive out the giants as the Lord said" (Joshua 14:6-14).

Like Caleb, in old age we should determine to meet the identity crisis at the present level. Such an attitude is a sign of good health. The wish to change our identity, to preserve and exercise a sense of possibility and incompleteness against a sense of closure and completeness, is an indication one is still filled with the desire for living.

No adult is as mature as he can be. Maturity is a continuing process throughout life, a process of becoming. Paul acknowledged he had not yet become mature or achieved the goals set before him, but he was still pressing on toward the goal in Christ Jesus. The virtues or fruits of the Spirit, which are really gift-graces from God, include: love, joy, peace, longsuffering, gentleness, goodness, faith, meekness, temperance (Gal. 5:22-24). These inner qualities should become the primary concern of the mature person.

As I grow older, I find that faith is a reality I cannot get along without. It is God's gift by which I can open the door of my life and receive him and all his gifts. By faith I have been redeemed, and by faith I have received all the grace-gifts that have enriched life. Martin Luther said, "I know not the way he leads me, but well do I know my guide. What have

I to fear?" I am learning with Paul that "we walk by faith and not by sight" (2 Cor. 5:7).

Faith is more than feeling. I was visiting a woman who was deeply depressed because she was confined to her bed by illness. She had tried to exercise faith, but it seemed to no avail. I shared with her a statement I learned many years ago: "When I cannot exercise the faith of assurance, I can still exercise the faith of adherence." She asked, "Will you please write that out on a card and leave it with me? I need a lesson in faith."

Contentment is another virtue I need to cultivate. Paul was in prison when he wrote, "I have learned in whatsoever circumstances I am to be content" (Phil. 4:11). He had to learn how to be content by purposeful intention, by discipline, and by dependence upon the Lord. The prayer written by Reinhold Niebuhr has blessed my own life: "Lord, give us the serenity to accept the things we cannot change, courage to change the things we can, and wisdom to know the one from the other."

Mrs. Hamilton, who is now in a nursing home, shared her feelings one day as we visited together: "This is not like being in my own home. At first, it was a strange environment with strange persons all around. However, I am learning to accept it and have found that I can be fairly content." Her eighty-year-old roommate, busy crocheting a cover for a bright yellow pillow, added: "We really find a lot of satisfaction wherever we are in life, once we make up our minds to it."

Joy is also one of life's greatest gifts. Man is created to be joyful, and he can experience joy in all of life's activities if he will cultivate it. Joy is found at the deeper levels of life. It is not dependent upon circumstances, certainly not upon any particular age level. Throughout life, even during old age, we can experience joy. Joy awakens a new interest in the world, in the concrete realities of every day—in the beauty of a rose, the fragrance of a perfume, the song of a gifted vocalist, the learning of a new fact, the love of another person. The joy of each moment is unique, something I never experienced before and shall never experience again.

I have found semi-retirement a time for celebration. At this stage of life, there are forms of joy I have never before experienced in the same way. I find a new sense of joy in my children and grandchildren, and in a maturing companionship of nearly forty years with my beloved wife. I take delight in certain achievements in my own life. I see the world of 1975 as a new adventure.

Christ said the life of a Christian should abound in joy: "These things I have spoken to you, that my joy may be in you and that your joy may be full" (John 15:11). Paul challenged his fellow Christians, "Rejoice in the Lord always; again I say, Rejoice" (Phil. 4:4). Paul found joy because of God's blessings upon him, and he found joy in spite of the trials that beset him.

Hope is another of the Christian's rich assets. Hope is the constant expectation that God will fulfill all that he has promised. It points toward the goal of eternal redemption and beckons man to persist in his expectations.

God is man's hope; therefore, man hopes in God. Hope is involved in both divine action and human response. God's promise for the future can be relied on, for his faithful and steadfast love guarantees the fulfillment of his Word. Because hope is God-grounded, God-sustained, and God-directed, it is a reality within which men live.

Hope is a living bond between the believer and God. Man experiences hope by faith. What we have already received gives us confidence that God has much more in store for us.

Hope is based upon the victory of Jesus Christ in his death

and resurrection. Jesus is the assurance of the promise in God's eternal purposes. The writer of Hebrews said, "We look unto him who is the pioneer and perfecter of our faith" (Heb. 12:2).

Hope enables us to participate in life's greatest and last adventure. The resurrection is a new departure, a leap into a new adventure. The adventure of hope begins in our salvation, it is renewed in fellowship with Jesus Christ, it is strengthened by God's Spirit in the face of trials, and it promises a full share in the life with God which never ends.

Jesus firmed up the hope of his disciples in his final discourse: "Let not your hearts be troubled. You trust in God, trust in me also. In my Father's house there are many rooms. If it were not so, I should have told you, for I am going to prepare a place for you. And if I go and prepare a place for you, I will return and will take you to be with me, so that where I am you may be also. And the way is known to you all, where I am going. . . . I am the Way, the Truth and the Life. . . . Peace I leave with you. My own peace I give to you. . . . Let not your heart be troubled, neither let it be afraid" (John 14:1-4,6,27, *Centenary Translation*).

To be alive and past sixty-five is a gift from God! May the years that lie ahead for all of us be filled with joy and challenge. At least, we can dedicate and offer them up to our Creator, who works for good in all things with those who love him. If he is for us, we can go forward with confidence. Let us stay alive to life during our earthly pilgrimage with our minds focused always on the Creator who is completing our lives eternally.

Notes

Chapter 1

1. "The Easter Perspective," a sermon by John R. Claypool, April 22, 1973.
2. *Learn to Grow Old* (New York: Harper and Row, 1971), p. 9.
3. James Alfred Peterson, *Married Love in the Middle Years* (New York: Association Press, 1968).
4. Herbert Shore, ed., *Adventures in Group Living* (Dallas: Golden Acres, 1972).
5. Ethel Sabin Smith, *The Dynamics of Aging* (New York: W. W. Norton, 1956), p. 189.
6. Ross Snyder, *On Becoming Human* (Nashville: Abingdon Press, 1967).
7. Albert Rosenfeld, "The Longevity Seekers," *Saturday Review of the Sciences*, Mar. 1973, pp. 46-51.

Chapter 2

1. William D. Poe, *The Old Person in Your Home* (New York: Charles Scribner's Sons, 1969), p. 21.
2. Lewis J. Sherrill, *The Struggle of the Soul* (New York: Macmillan, 1951), p. 198.
3. Op cit, pp. 22-23.

Chapter 3

1. *The Adventure of Living* (New York: Harper and Row, 1965).

Chapter 4

1. Alfons Deeken, *Growing Old and How to Cope with It* (New York: Paulist Press, 1972).

2. Edward M. McGhee and Marvin D. Veronee, "Stages in Retirement," *The Christian Ministry,* Jan. 1974.

3. (Nashville: Abingdon Press, 1971).

4. Clark Tibbets, ed., "Retirement: The Emerging Social Pattern," *Handbook of Social Gerontology* (Chicago: University of Chicago Press, 1960), p. 378.

5. *To Understand Each Other* (Richmond: John Knox Press, 1969), p. 50.

6. Eva Schindler-Raiman, ed., *The Volunteer Community: Creative Use of Human Resources* (Washington: NTL Learning Resources, 1971), p. 1.

Chapter 5

1. Op cit, pp. 113-14.

2. (Nashville: Abingdon Press, 1969).

3. Appropriate passages of Scripture for visitation and counseling may be found in the closing section of my book *The Broadman Minister's Manual* (Nashville: Broadman Press, 1968).

4. *The Power to Bless* (Nashville: Abingdon Press, 1970), p. 151.

Chapter 6

1. *Reality-Orientation* (Washington: Hospital and Community Psychiatric Service); also, James C. Folsom, "Reality-Orientation for the Elderly Mental Patient," *Journal of Geriatric Psychiatry,* Spring 1968.

Chapter 7

1. E. Mansell Pattison, "Afraid to Die," *Pastoral Psychology,* June 1972, pp. 41 ff.

2. Richard W. Voss, "Toward a Theology of Death," *Pastoral Psychology.* June 1972, pp. 15 ff.

3. *The Art of Dying* (New York: Harper and Row, 1971).

4. (New York: Macmillan, 1971).

5. J. William Word, "The Right to Die," *Pastoral Psychology,* June 1972.

6. Robert H. Williams, "The End of Life in the Elderly," *Post Graduate Medicine,* Dec. 1973, pp. 55 ff.

7. *The Christian Funeral* (New York: Channel Press, 1966).

Chapter 8

1. (New York: Chemical Publishing Co., 1972).

2. *Time,* Feb. 18, 1974.